A PENGUIN SPECIAL

ECOLOGY OF DEVASTATION:
INDOCHINA

John Lewallen was graduated from Whitman College, Walla Walla, Washington, in 1964, taking a degree in political science. He went on to become a Fulbright Tutor in English at the University of Rajasthan in India, and, while there, made a lengthy study of overall development in a Rajasthani village. After a year at Stanford Law School and a few months with a social science research corporation, he joined International Voluntary Services. From 1967 to 1969, he was an IVS development volunteer in a South Vietnamese district town, working on self-help projects and refugee relief, and learning the Vietnamese and Raglai Montagnard languages. In early 1971, Lewallen became Features Editor of *Clear Creek* magazine, a national environmental monthly. He says, "My life is writing, wielding words to seek and promote new perspectives on war and human ecology."

John Lewallen

Ecology
of Devastation:
Indochina

PENGUIN BOOKS INC
Baltimore · Maryland

Penguin Books Inc
7110 Ambassador Road
Baltimore, Maryland 21207, U.S.A.

First published 1971
Copyright © John J. Lewallen, 1971

Manufactured by Kingsport Press, Inc.,
Kingsport, Tennessee

Set in Monotype Bell

Library of Congress Catalog Card Number 79-176108

For Pennfield Jensen,
who took me to the library.

Acknowledgments

Among the many people who have helped me write this book by clarifying thought, supplying information, or reading portions of the manuscript are E. W. Pfeiffer of the University of Montana; Barry Weisberg of the Bay Area Institute in San Francisco; Peter Cohen, Bruce Bartholomew, and Patrice Morrow of Stanford University; Peter Hale of the University of California at Davis; Polly Roberts of the Center for Study of Responsive Law; and Linda Hess. My reliance on the work of many newsmen, scientists, and philosophers will be apparent to the reader. My mother, Mrs. Grace H. Lewallen, typed the final draft. Some of the above will be happy to read that the author is solely responsible for the contents of the book.

Berkeley, February 1971

Contents

	PAGE
INTRODUCTION	11

CHAPTER

1 FRACTURED SPIRIT, TEMPERED BLADE — 15
   Mountain Tribes and Valley Kingdoms
   South Vietnam: Draining the Insurging Seas
   Laos: The Subterranean Environment
   Cambodia: FARK versus FUNK
   Saigon: Fractured Spirit
   North Vietnam: Tempered Blade

2 THE GREEN DEVOLUTION — 58
   Operation Ranch Hand (Hades)
   Hushed Mangroves
   Spreading the Green Desert
   Crop Destruction
   Land Deform in the Mekong Delta

3 WAR UPON THE ANIMALS — 95

4 THE LUNARIZATION PROGRAM — 103

5 AIRS, WATERS, AND PLACES: ENVIRONMENTS OF DISEASE — 110
   Poisons from the Airs
   Stagnant Waters and Unhealthy Places
   The Last of the Raglai

6 ENVIRONMENTS OF TECHNOCRATIC WAR — 128
   Technocracy at War
   Energy Sources
   The Spectrum of Threats

7 SWITCHBOARD DEVASTATION — 146

NOTES 155
INDEX 169

LIST OF TABLES

Table 1: Composition and Characteristics of Military Herbicides — 64

Table 2: US Defense Department and NLF Estimates of Areas Sprayed with Herbicides in South Vietnam — 66

Table 3: Forest Areas of South Vietnam — 73

Table 4: Percentage of Desiccation and Defoliation Resulting from Herbicides Applied as Low-Volume Aerial Sprays on Rain-Forest Vegetation — 76

Introduction

Armies intent upon devastating the environment that supports human life are not new to Southeast Asia. In the twelfth and thirteenth centuries, what is now the jungle-twined ruin of Angkor in central Cambodia was the core of the powerful Khmer empire. During that era the empire's eastern borders were threatened by the aggressive Chams whose kingdom, Champa, lay in the harsh, confining valleys of coastal central Vietnam. In 1177 the Chams pushed up the Mekong River in a fleet of ferociously adorned rowboats and sacked Angkor after a battle similar to the eternal Cham-Khmer struggle carved in bas-relief on the walls of Angkor Wat. The Khmers rebounded from disgrace and mounted a series of invasions with infantry and elephants, which led to the defeat of Champa in 1203.

The invading Khmer and Cham armies saw as their culminating act of conquest the destruction of the linga of the god-king. At the center of each civilization was a linga representing the Hindu god Shiva. Placed on a religiously significant hill and ceremoniously invested with the very essence of the king, the linga was considered to be the source of all royal power and authority, and to regulate the rhythm of the monsoon. This phallic rock was the focus of an interdependent system of temples, irrigation works, and human duties. By smashing the linga of their enemy, the invading armies sought to loose anarchy and the vengeance of the elements upon the defeated population.

Historians judge that the Khmer empire decayed not as a result of acts of symbolic environmental castration, but partially because wars and extensive temple construction caused the Khmers to neglect their intricate irrigation system. Siamese armies, attacking Angkor from the west in the fourteenth century, blocked the irrigation canals. Denied a recurrent covering of fertile river silt, the lateritic soils in the Angkor area hardened and became barren. In 1432, probably after a destructive flood, Angkor's inhabitants abandoned their city and scattered to farm alluvial plains. When the

ECOLOGY OF DEVASTATION: INDOCHINA

French discovered the awesome structures of Angkor in the nineteenth century, they found that the Cambodians believed that a race of semi-divine giants, rather than their Khmer ancestors, had raised these edifices.

Beginning in the tenth century, the Vietnamese, pushing southward from the Red River valley, slaughtered many of the Chams and absorbed the rest into their dynamic culture. Eventually, only a few villages of Chams, clinging to ancient customs, remained of the Champa kingdom. Establishing colonies in the Mekong River delta, the Vietnamese were gradually encroaching upon Khmer territory and culture when the French arrested this process in the nineteenth century. If assaults upon human environment are not new to Southeast Asia, neither are policies of systematic cultural annihilation.

The interrelated wars currently sweeping Vietnam, Cambodia, and Laos—the countries that formerly made up French Indochina—do not owe their uniqueness to the destructive intentions of the combatants. A historian looking back on the Second Indochina War is unlikely to find any outstanding brutality on any side. The programs and motives of the contestants, which presently dominate thinking about Indochina, will appear drearily familiar in the future. What will stand out as the unique feature of the Second Indochina War is that it marks mankind's first wartime use of technological power to devastate the living environment of Earth.

It is well-known that ecological damage is a by-product of industrial production. But in Indochina, environmental destruction is not a troublesome side effect of technology. It is an intended result. The United States Government and the sundry regimes it supports in Indochina are striving to defeat their enemies by altering environments.

Foliage that gives the enemy cover has been chemically destroyed. Food crops thought to belong to the enemy have been sprayed with poisons. The industries, transportation networks, dikes, and villages of North Vietnam have been bombed in an attempt to cut the enemies off from their supplies and to crush their will. The human communities of Indochina—the towns and villages from which the enemies arise, which keep the enemies alive, and which the enemies seek to dominate politically—are being forcibly imploded into urban aggregations, which the United States and its allies hope they can control. Great swaths of territory are being laid waste by B-52 bombers, with such scant hope of damaging the enemy that one can only consider these raids frustrated flailings at the land itself, at the home of an elusive enemy who fights with undimmed fury although his environment is being torn down around him.

The Second Indochina War is a war of broad ecological dimensions, so an ecological perspective is necessary to understand it. Ecology, a word derived from the Greek *oikos* (house), is the study of natural structure and function. It is clear that the strategies and weapons employed in the Second Indochina War are changing the household of life—the ecosystem—of Indochina.

The environmental changes being wrought by the conflict cannot be fully described or predicted at present, because of a lack of data. Nevertheless it is important to begin an inquiry into the ecological dynamics of the war, for ecology instructs us that events in the biosphere, the thin shell of life enveloping the Earth, are closely interrelated. Ecological tragedy in Indochina is a tragedy we must all share and is a continuing tragedy over which each of us has a little control.

At the center of concern are the people directly affected by the war. The opening chapter is a wide-angle view of the effects of the war on the patterns of human life in Indochina. In studying the effects of the war on the natural environment, emphasis is placed on changes in those natural elements that support people, keeping in mind that *all* ecological changes are subtly and often mysteriously related to human welfare. In brief, the following chapters constitute a study of the human ecology of the Second Indochina War.

The inquiry into the war's effects on the natural environment is also focused on what ecologists often term (using an appropriately military metaphor) "trigger factors." Trigger factors are those elements injected into an environment that touch off widespread ecological changes. An exemplary trigger factor is 2,4,5-T, a defoliant chemical that has been applied to the forests of Vietnam. In strong enough concentrations, 2,4,5-T causes the leaves to fall off trees and the trees to die. A web of consequences may then result in the replacement of a tropical rain forest with the relatively life-poor ecology of a tropical savanna. In addition, 2,4,5-T directly affects human health in ways not fully understood and may cause birth defects. A chemical intended to merely expose an enemy to view may trigger ecological changes, which unfold over decades or even centuries.

The impact of military trigger factors on the plant life, animal life, and nonliving physical aspects of the Indochinese environment is also considered. One chapter specifically views the effects of the war, in terms of the chemicals it unleashes and the organisms it encourages, on the health of the Indochinese peoples.

Two concluding chapters examine the human organizations that carry out the American portion of the Indochina war. One of these chapters studies the American military-industrial complex as a living system, with interdependent elements relating to one another much as natural elements do in an ecosystem. This meld of sociology and ecology, it is hoped, will contribute to clearer understanding of the organizational mechanisms that drive the United States forward in Indochina. The final chapter offers a look at the future of the Second Indochina War and at the future environments of Indochina.

This book is intended to be a preliminary approach to the ecology of devastation. If ecology is, in the words of Paul B. Sears, "the subversive science," and if it has replaced economics as "the dismal science," then the ecological analysis of the mechanisms of technological war and their devastating environmental effects must surely be the most dismal and subversive inquiry of all. I hope I have approached this study with the attitudes man should use in meeting his environment: caution, humility, and sensitivity to consequence.

CHAPTER ONE

Fractured Spirit, Tempered Blade

Is it possible to speak of the ecology of modern humanity?

Ecologists often divide the natural world into three levels of integration: the individual, the population, and the ecosystem. A tiger, for example, may be studied as an individual interacting with its environment. Or a local tiger population, consisting of a relatively isolated, interbreeding group of individual tigers, may be observed in relation to its environment. Tiger individuals and populations are also integrated into ecosystems, which are living systems involving many plants, animals, and physical elements. Ecologists boldly strive to delineate a whole ecosystem, such as a tropical savanna of which tigers are only a small part. But ecosystems are unbounded. Endless lines of biological relationship and energy-flow attach to the tropical savanna and enmesh the individual tiger in the fate of the universe.

Ecology, a concept easily understood, is an extremely complex field of study. A bewildering set of factors links the individual tiger to his environment. As the ecologist's inquiry expands to the population and ecosystem, the variables grow to literally astronomical proportions. It is no wonder that ecologists are notorious for saying that everything needs more study.

If tiger ecology is a complicated study, how much more difficult is the study of human ecology! Men are involved not only in the natural environment, but also in cultural oceans. They are immersed in political, economic, and social milieus, bound to artifacts of their own making. They not only live in the biosphere, but through the operation of rational thought, have created what Pierre Teilhard de Chardin termed the noösphere, which is the sphere of conscious invention that is the unique home of mankind.

Modern science has sought to cope with the complexity of man and his environment by separating the fields of inquiry. The study of natural science is severed from the study of social science, disciplines such as biophysics and political science are carved out of the whole, specific problems are tightly defined and systematically attacked. The application of the scientific method to delineate problems has led to an understanding of natural phenomena and to the use of this understanding to invent the technological devices that largely determine the quality of modern life.

It is increasingly realized that the divisions of science are artificial and that the subject matter of all science is interrelated. The divisions of science are not only artificial, they are dangerous. For although the limited scientist may be able to see in detail the cribbed problem before him, often he cannot see its relation to the whole of reality. When society makes decisions on the basis of fragmentary scientific studies, it often acts blindly, lashing out at chimeras that exist only within the narrow frames of so-called problem areas.

In the mid-sixties I worked briefly for a social science research corporation located near Washington, D.C. Some members of that corporation, social scientists, were hot at work on Southeast Asian studies under contract to the Defense Department. Many of these studies were in the budding field of counterinsurgency. It soon came clear that, to a student of Southeast Asian counterinsurgency, Indochina was three governments threatened by insurgents. Counterinsurgent thinking proceeded from this mind fix. By reference to other so-called insurgencies, such as the Huk movement in the Philippines and the communist anti-colonial rebellion in British Malaya, the counterinsurgent scholar of that day sought ways to destroy the Indochinese insurgent's life-support system. The counterinsurgent scientists were striving to define the ecology of the insurgent in order to find the means to eradicate him.

As I shall be at some pains to explain in this chapter, there are no real insurgents in Indochina. Counterinsurgency is a pseudoscience, which has limited its vision to such degree that it has created paper creatures lurking in a triple-canopy jargon jungle. The creations of counterinsurgents would be as harmless as the Hobbits of Tolkien if the American military machine had not been dispatched to annihilate them. Unfortunately, there are real rebels in Indochina. American counterinsurgency tactics, smashing at the environment of mythical insurgents, produce rebels much faster than they destroy them.

The counterinsurgency programs used in the Second Indochina War offer devastating evidence of the danger of limited science. The very fracturing of world view that makes possible the invention of bombers and electronic sweat-sniffers has, to a great extent, directed America's weaponry to tasks of mindless, repetitive destruction. In the Indochina war we see science gone mad, metaphorically acting out aggressions and unable to respond to the real world.

Is there a holistic science, a discipline that can view man and environment as a whole? Furthermore, can it guide human action?

F. Fraser Darling, a pioneer in the application of ecological science to studying human society, has offered broad but useful guidelines for the study of human ecology:

> In human ecology we can never neglect history, for we are studying process; I would say, therefore, that a cross-sectional social survey is not ecological unless it studies origins and successions, in other words, process. We must always remember the significance of political action as an environmental factor. . . .
>
> The science of ecology deals with causes of observed biological phenomena, and it should be expected to lay bare multiple-factor causation, which is a very difficult field. But

it is also concerned with consequences and ramifications. The practical value of ecology, as I have said, is the ability to forecast consequences of certain courses of action and of observable trends. The politician has to be very careful here, and I would suggest that the ecologist is as necessary a servant to the statesman as the economist.

Darling distrusts the use of opinion questionnaires, especially when seeking truth among strangers who have good reason to lie:

> Much the best way is observation and soaking in the culture. Ability to observe closely and interpret accurately, by way of a large grasp of the organism of a society in its habitat, is the essence of human ecology. It is an integrative science as much as an analytical one, with observation as its basis. . . . Teamwork in human ecology will be essential, but still each specialist will have to have the quality of delighting in another man's work and linking his own to it; and he cannot be the traditionally remote academic type, but must be inquisitive about what humankind is doing to itself.

In this book, ecology is employed as a holistic perspective to the Indochina war. This chapter describes the human cultures of Indochina and analyzes the impact of American people, tactics, and weaponry on those cultures. The scope of this look at the peoples of Indochina cuts through traditional boundaries of disciplined science. Often determinants lack constants, and the material included has been shaped by what I have read and experienced. In other words, ecology as used here is not a science; it is a perspective. I hope that readers of this perspective will strive to develop, rather than fragment, a science of human ecology.

Mountain Tribes and Valley Kingdoms

Indochina dangles like a tortured appendix from the Asian landmass. Most of its 286,000 square miles are composed of hills and mountains. Laos is all mountainous, except for the Mekong River valley and a few elevated plateaus, notably the Plain of Jars in the north and the Bolovens plateau in the south. Cambodia is a broad plain lying between mountain ranges on the northeast and southwest. The two Vietnams are often likened to a pair of rice baskets dangling from a pole: the baskets are the Red River valley in the north and the Mekong River delta in the south; the pole is the chain of small coastal valleys feeding from the hills of the Annam Cordillera. All of Indochina lies south of the Tropic of Cancer, and men and nature are regulated by the tempo of the monsoons.

Indochina is the adopted home of many ethnic groups. It is a land of immigrants, both of early colonists who migrated from Indonesia and, more recently, of tribes moving down from China. Its history is one of continual conflict for control of territory, a struggle shaped by the region's physical and cultural geography. The ethnic wars of Indochina are far from being past history. Rather, they are the true "secret wars" of Indochina, invisible to Western eyes bedazzled by the clash of ideology and great power.

The river valleys of Indochina have always supported the dominant kingdoms of the region and the economic base of these kingdoms has always been the cultivation of paddy rice. The Khmer and Cham civilizations grew by using irrigation techniques learned from Indian Hindus. The Vietnamese kingdom in the Red River valley developed by adopting Chinese paddy-farming methods.

Vietnam remained in the Red River valley during the period it was administered as a Chinese province, a phase that lasted roughly one thousand years. After finally throwing the Chinese out in the tenth century, the Vietnamese pushed southward. Vietnamese expansion was concentrated in the coastal river valleys of central Vietnam, environments where they could practice paddy-rice cultivation. These valleys were the homes of the Chams, whose kingdom was finished off by the Vietnamese in 1471.

During the thirteenth and fourteenth centuries, the Siamese (or Thais) established a kingdom in the Chao Phraya River basin to the northwest of Cambodia. In the fourteenth century, a people who came to be known as the Lao founded the kingdom of Lan Xang in the upper valley of the Mekong

ECOLOGY OF DEVASTATION: INDOCHINA

River. Both Siam and Lan Xang expanded at the expense of the Khmer empire, which ceased to exist in the fifteenth century.

By the mid-nineteenth century, just prior to the French colonization of Indochina, the shape of the present conflicts among the paddy-farming civilizations could be seen. Lan Xang had broken into three impotent kingdoms located in what is now Laos. The Khmers, their military power spent, were farming the Mekong River delta and the lands around the huge lake called Tonle Sap, in central Cambodia. Two powerful and expansive civilizations, Vietnam and Siam, were fighting for control of Laos and Cambodia, which lay between them.

The wars among the valley kingdoms of Indochina have involved the upland expanses as well as the paddy-farming regions. In order to understand the relations between mountain tribes and valley peoples in Indochina, it is essential to examine the topography and ecology of the region.

The ethnic groups of Indochina have the fascinating characteristic of being adapted to life at specific elevations. An ethnographic map of the region is a topographic map as well. Vietnamese, for example, rarely settled in areas above 500 feet in elevation until very recent times. Other tribes, such as the Muong of North Vietnam and the Mon-Khmer upland tribes of the Annam Cordillera, are found at higher elevations, ranging from the upper river valleys to an altitude of about 3,000 feet. The Meos in North Vietnam and Laos choose to live only above 3,000 feet.

Slash-and-burn, or swidden, agriculture is the traditional base of upland tribal economies. Swidden agriculture involves cutting forest foliage, spreading it on the soil, and burning it. The burning unlocks the nutrients stored in the living forest foliage. Diverse crops, with rice normally predominating, are then planted in the ash-covered soil of the clearing, to await the waters of the monsoon. The swidden crop, with its diversity and evaporation-retarding canopy of leafy plants, is in many respects an imitation of forest ecology.

As discussed more fully in Chapter 2, most of the nutrients

of a tropical forest are contained in its living matter. Tropical soils are poor in humus. To the swidden agriculturist, this means that his soil is rapidly exhausted and he must abandon the clearing, or field, after a few years. If the field is left in good time, secondary forest will spring up and he can come back to slash, burn, and plant it again. However, if the swidden field is farmed too long or too frequently, the soil degrades until it will no longer support forest growth. It may then become completely barren. Or it may become "green desert," covered with savanna grass and unsuitable for cultivation.

A population increase among swidden farmers tends to cause premature recultivation of plots. This tendency is accelerated by the fact that it is very hard work to cut down virgin forest with simple tools, so swidden farmers prefer to slash the secondary growth on used land. An expanding or inefficient swidden-farming population may destroy the environment that supports it. (The Meos of Laos, to be examined later, are a striking example of destructive swidden agriculturists.)

Swidden agriculture, then, can support only a small number of people. By contrast, paddy-rice cultivation, with a far greater yield per acre, can feed large populations living in close geographical proximity. Furthermore, the pressure of growing population does not destroy paddy-rice land. Paddy rice receives most of its nutrition from irrigation water, which is the medium of its growth, rather than from the soil. Paddy cultivators can increase the intensity of land use and refine growing techniques to increase yield. As long as the rich waters flow, the paddy field will remain productive.

The paddy-farming alluvial plains of Indochina make up about 13 percent of the region's land area, but support more than 85 percent of its population. Before the coming of the French, the lowland cultures were confined to these plains. The lowland peoples would fight one another for the tribute of mountain tribes and for control of mountain territory. They would carry slaves from the uplands to the lowlands. But they never settled or cultivated the highlands. The mountain tribes

ECOLOGY OF DEVASTATION: INDOCHINA

remained at their respective elevations practicing swidden agriculture, most of them hoping that the lowlanders would leave them to the peace of solitude.

The French, who began colonizing Indochina in 1858, had a profound effect on this dynamic system of cultures and on the relations between cultures and natural environments. In 1864 they established a protectorate over Cambodia, thereby halting the Siamese-Vietnamese struggle for military control of that country. In 1893, they blockaded Bangkok and forced Siam to cede Laos, which became a French protectorate. This gave the French control of the territory that imperial Vietnam had previously claimed as its sphere of influence.

Vietnam had been divided among three warring regional kingdoms until the early nineteenth century. Now it was again split into three administrative units, this time by the French: the protectorate of Tonkin (North Vietnam), the protectorate of Annam in central Vietnam, and the wholly French-governed colony of Cochin China in the Mekong River delta region. The French introduced sweeping reforms in lowland Vietnamese society. By contrast, they left the feudal and tribal cultures of Cambodia and Laos relatively untouched, although they did use Vietnamese to staff their colonial apparatus there. The French governed the central highlands of Vietnam themselves and prevented the lowland Vietnamese from coming into close contact with the mountain tribes.

An agricultural revolution was fostered by the French in Indochina. The irrigation system in the Red River delta was improved to control flooding. By draining swamps and developing irrigation channels, the French converted the Mekong delta into a vast quilt of rice paddies. Chemical fertilizer was introduced. New crops were brought in, most notably rubber and coffee, which were cultivated in large plantations on land previously good only for swidden agriculture. The cultivation of tea, a local crop, was improved and organized into plantations. These agricultural innovations were confined almost exclusively to what are now the two Vietnams and also to southeastern Cambodia, where rubber plantations were established.

Between 1861 and 1937 the population of what are now the Vietnams increased by 270 percent. By 1945, the year that most Vietnamese think of as the beginning of a war not yet terminated, Indochina was on the verge of explosive changes in the relations among peoples and ecosystems. From the French, the Vietnamese had learned agricultural techniques that produced rich yields from the highlands and that, at the same time, restored soil nutrients and prevented ecological deterioration. The French had also taught them the concept of a modern nation-state and had fitted them into the colonial administrative structure. The days of tribal isolation in the highlands and of feudal stagnation in the valleys of Cambodia and Laos were numbered.

The Japanese had become the controlling power in Indochina in 1940. But the Vichy French colonial bureaucracy was allowed to continue functioning until March 9, 1945, when the Japanese swiftly disarmed the local French forces and arrested the French officials. On March 11, after meeting with the Japanese ambassador, the Annamese emperor Bao Dai declared Vietnam independent of the French. This left a political vacuum, which was filled when the Viet Minh, nationalist and communist revolutionaries who had been organizing for a long while, bloodlessly took Hanoi on August 19. Shortly thereafter, the Viet Minh leader, Ho Chi Minh, accepted the imperial seal from Bao Dai. Saigon and much of the countryside of what is now South Vietnam soon fell under Viet Minh administration. After World War II ended in September, French reinforcements landed in Indochina to reassert French colonial rights and the First Indochina War was engaged.

From beginning to end, the war between the Viet Minh and the French involved the highlands and the mountain tribesmen. The first Viet Minh offensive, which took the mountainous northern part of North Vietnam from the French in 1950, was fought largely by native Tho tribesmen. In 1951 the Viet Minh military commander, Vo Nguyen Giap, launched a "general counteroffensive" against the French in the Red River valley. This offensive ended with the disastrous defeat of the Viet Minh, who could not match French firepower in the lowlands. Thereafter the Viet Minh fought in the highlands, drawing the French into hill engagements from central Vietnam to Laos. The final battle of the war was joined at Dien Bien Phu, in a high valley in the mountains of North Vetnam. In 1954, its will broken by the crushing defeat at Dien Bien Phu, France signed the Geneva Convention, which partitioned Vietnam at the 17th Parallel. The remaining French forces withdrew from the region and left the wars of Indochina to its native peoples—and to the Americans.

In order to join forces with mountain tribesmen on their own land, the Vietnamese of the Viet Minh had to overcome the centuries-old hatred of highlander for lowlander. They also had to overcome traditional Vietnamese fear and loathing of mountain men, who were widely believed to be animals or dark and deadly spirits. The Viet Minh assigned cadres to marry into the various tribes and to respectfully study tribal customs, a revolutionary departure from the traditional Vietnamese policies of genocide and forced cultural assimilation. After the establishment of the Democratic Republic of Vietnam (DRV) in North Vietnam, two "autonomous zones" were created in the mountain tribal areas of the northeastern and northwestern parts of the republic. These zones, the DRV announced, would be under central government administration, but their various governmental services would be staffed by local tribesmen. A Central Minorities School was set up in Hanoi to train teachers and political cadres for mountain tribes throughout Indochina. An estimated 10,000 tribesmen from the highlands of South Vietnam went north in 1954 to learn to write and to study their various languages in the Latinized script developed by the Viet Minh.

The government of South Vietnam, under Ngo Dinh Diem, took a quite different view of "their" mountains and Montagnards (a generic term for the many tribes of the central highlands). They saw with the eyes of a nineteenth-century white American looking at the Wild West: sweeps of virgin, untamed land infested with threatening savages who existed without benefit of (Vietnamese) civilization. Vietnamese merchants moved into the highlands of South Vietnam. Early in 1957 the South Vietnamese Government (GVN) began establishing *agrovilles* in the central highlands. These resettlement communities were intended to absorb Vietnamese refugees who had migrated from the north in 1954, to build a defensive chain of people loyal to the GVN, and to open "uninhabited" land to cultivation. Garden crops and fibers (jute and ramie) were to support the economies of these settlements. Robert Scigliano estimated that between 1957 and the early 1960s, more than 210,000 Vietnamese were settled in 147 *agrovilles* carved out of 220,000 acres of "wilderness."

But what was wilderness to the GVN was and is home to the swidden-farming mountain tribes. They see themselves as facing massive invasion and displacement by the hated Vietnamese. South Vietnamese creation of an ethnic minorities service, under various names, has been widely regarded by the Montagnards as a cover for cultural genocide. The few Montagnard officials holding high GVN office have been seen by their fellow tribesmen as dull-witted lackeys of the *Yuan* (Vietnamese) rather than true Montagnard leaders.

Into this swamp of cultural conflict rushed the Americans. The first American military aid in Indochina was given by the Office of Strategic Services (OSS)—a forerunner of the Central Intelligence Agency (CIA)—to anti-Japanese forces under the leadership of Ho Chi Minh. By 1950, however, Ho Chi Minh and his troops were viewed by the US government as part of the so-called Red Menace. Consequently, US supplies began flowing to the French in Indochina. American involvement in Indochina then grew cancerously. The effects of the Americans on the region's ethnic groups, in relation to one another and to their environments, have been of two broad types: the uprooting of cultures from their natural environments and the arming of tribal chauvinist movements. These effects have complemented each other. Every day that the war continues, noncommunist Indochina increasingly becomes a world of peoples torn from their homelands and conditioned to relate with other cultures by waging total war.

ECOLOGY OF DEVASTATION: INDOCHINA

The dynamics of what Americans in Indochina call "generating and processing refugees" will be examined in detail later. An analysis of the way the United States is creating tribal armies throughout, and beyond, Indochina may well begin with a look at the central highlands of South Vietnam, where I worked with both lowland and mountain peoples from early 1967 to early 1969.

Of the estimated 15 to 18 million people living in South Vietnam (excluding Americans and allies called "third-country nationals"), about 1,000,000 are of Chinese descent, 500,000 in the Mekong delta are of Cambodian descent, and some one million are Montagnards in the central highlands.

South Vietnam's Montagnards have not lacked contact with the mountain peoples to the north. By 1957 Montagnards and Vietnamese cadres were infiltrating the central highlands from North Vietnam. In mid-1961 there were 2,500-man National Liberation Front (NFL) Montagnard regiments operating at full strength in the highlands. By 1963 all four of the Montagnard regiments that had fought with the Viet Minh against the French had been reactivated in the area. These units were fighting for the same arrangement of autonomous zones within a communist state that the mountain peoples of North Vietnam had already achieved.

The French, in fighting the Viet Minh, had formed all-Montagnard units under French command. In essence, this policy had put a white buffer between Montagnards and Vietnamese. The Americans and the Saigon government lunged forward along the path cut by the French. In the early sixties, the US Special Forces (initially under CIA control) began forming Montagnard units, usually in battalion strength. By 1962 there were 36 so-called Mike Force units of Montagnards under the Special Forces. In 1963 the Special Forces took over a CIA-financed collection of battalions, many of them all-Montagnard units. These were called Civilian Irregular Defense Groups (CIDG). Later the Truong Son cadre program was established. Under the GVN's ethnic minorities service but financed by the CIA, the Truong Son Montagnards were trained in a school in Pleiku both to secure and to foster development projects in their home villages. In 1967 the CIA created Provincial Reconnaissance Units (PRUs), which were 55-man teams under the command of Americans or white mercenaries. Their main job was to eliminate the NLF's shadow-government members. Many PRUs were all-Montagnard units.

The South Vietnamese Army (ARVN) has offered little to attract Montagnards. Montagnards are not subject to the national draft, although they may be impressed into local militias. It is impossible for Montagnards to attain high rank in the ARVN; by contrast, there are mountain tribesmen at the general officer level in the North Vietnamese Army. Furthermore, the ARVN pays less than do the American-created Montagnard units. As a result, Mike Force and similar units are filled with Montagnard deserters from the ARVN.

The American-led Montagnard units have served to separate Montagnards both from NLF control and from GVN control, thereby laying the military basis for a full-fledged Montagnard independence movement. The GVN noticed that their big brothers the Americans were creating a new armed insurgency while they watched. So in 1964 they ordered all Montagnard units integrated into the ARVN. The Montagnards deserted in droves, killing many of their new Vietnamese commanders. In September 1964, Montagnard troops of Special Forces units massacred sixty Vietnamese officers in Ban Me Thuot. They briefly seized the town and proclaimed it independent under the three-starred flag of Fulro, the Montagnard independence movement.

The ARVN integration plan was scrapped and the Montagnard units led by Americans still exist at this writing. Violence frequently flares between these units and Vietnamese soldiers and civilians. In September 1965, there was another large rebellion by Mike Force Montagnards. At that time, the Fulro leader, Iba Ham, fled with a number of highland troops to set up headquarters in Cambodia. In 1968 I became aware that Fulro had an underground organization that penetrated throughout the Montagnard tribes of the highlands and also into the Cambodian community of the Mekong delta. Its headquarters was in Pnom Penh and it controlled a substantial number of troops. I saw a list of Fulro demands in which Fulro sought to negotiate with Saigon in "a neutral country" for control of its own regiments and management of its own ethnic minorities service throughout South Vietnam. The GVN regards Fulro as it does the NLF—as an enemy of the state.

The CIA, true to its image of trying to buy and arm everybody (including, at one time, your faithful reporter), soon began feeding guns and succor to Fulro. (A CIA agent told me in 1969 that he had given supplies to Fulro.) The dismal compulsions that drive CIA agents to arm all sides in the tribal wars of Indochina will be examined more fully in Chapter 6. The American aim in arming tribes is to enlist their ancient hatreds in the battle against communism. This policy invariably backfires against the American-supported lowland governments, for it empowers the most cynical and chauvinistic tribal leaders.

Americans who work with highland peoples commonly learn to love the tribes they work with and to adopt the tribal hatreds toward lowland peoples. This ethnic infatuation leads Americans to promise sundry tribes long-term support, which, of course, cannot be delivered. Many Americans work with hill tribes for years, joining their battle for cultural survival, only to realize in the end that they have prevented any peaceful compromise between the hill and valley peoples of Indochina. Perhaps a short definition of a modern American is a lonely warrior in search of his tribe.

As I write, the arming of ancient passions in Indochina proceeds apace. A recent development was uncovered by Michael Morrow of Dispatch News International, a bold young news-service headquartered in Saigon. According to Morrow's sources, the CIA has been aiding Shan tribesmen of the mountains of Burma in their rebellion against the Burmese Government. At the same time, the Burmese Government has been using an $85.5 million aid agreement negotiated with the United States in 1958 to build up its army, the better to put down the Shan, Mon, and Karen tribal uprisings. Just over every horizon there is always a virgin tribe, waiting for that clean-cut American toting a moneybag and struggling to master the dialect.

South Vietnam: Draining the Insurging Seas

"A guerrilla swims among the people as a fish swims in water." This marine metaphor, attributed to Mao Tse-tung, is the most famous aphorism of counterinsurgency. To the counterinsurgent, Indochina is a sea of people, where governments and insurgents compete for control of the human waters. Pursuing this metaphor, the counterinsurgent may seek to destroy the insurgent in three ways. First, the insurgent may be netted or speared like a fish. Second, the ecology of the insurgent's environment, which encompasses the people and resources on which he relies, may be altered so that it can longer support his life. Finally, the seas of mankind in which the insurgent exists may be drained, leaving him like a fish out of water.

The American counterinsurgency effort in Indochina has moved, in general, from emphasis on the first and second of these strategies to reliance on the third. Early attempts to identify and kill Indochinese rebels while at the same time trying to gain popular support for governments have given way to massive population relocations. As an observer of forced refugee movement in Laos put it recently, "If you can't take the government to the people, then you bring the people to the government."

The making of refugees out of the Indochinese peoples, a process that began during the First Indochina War, has profoundly altered the human cultures of the region. Before focusing on the cultural effects of "generating" refugees in specific regions, we may recall that nearly all the peoples of Indochina were agriculturists before the war began. Their economic ties to their home villages were great. Contrary to what is sometimes written, even most swidden farmers lived in long-established villages, using temporary camps when they had to cultivate distant fields. Also, Indochinese peoples were adapted to ecosystems at very specific elevations, and had worked out more-or-less stable cultural relationships with their neighbors.

Religion reinforces the relationship between the Indochinese and their natural environments. Despite the rich cultural diversity of the region, all Indochinese are animists. Most mountain tribes are purely animist, but the Vietnamese, Laotians, and Cambodians blend animism with Buddhism. Animists regard the trees, rivers, winds and all other natural elements as being animated by spirits. They hold ceremonies to appease dangerous spirits and to thank kindly spirits. They believe that man's use of his world is ordered by the presumed desires of the spirits lurking in the environment. Taking an animist from his home village to a refugee camp does far more than merely dislocate his economy and society; it assaults his view of the world and his identity in relation to his environment.

Each traditional Vietnamese Buddhist village has a *dinh*, which houses the chief spirit of the village. The worship of the chief spirit and of other village deities is regulated by a cult committee. Buddhist geomancers are called upon to make sure that houses, graves, and all other changes in the landscape are harmoniously oriented toward the five elements: wood, metal, fire, water, and earth.

Confucian ancestor-worship further attaches the Vietnamese Buddhist's total being to the village of his birth. Each house in the village has an ancestral shrine. Departed parents and grandparents are believed to hover formlessly about the house, making sure that their progeny are living good lives. The people believe that if they are not buried in their home villages, with the aid of a geomancer, their spirits will wander without rest and their children will be cursed. (Vietnamese bus companies, capitalizing on this custom, charge staggering rates for transporting bodies.)

Because most South Vietnamese are Buddhists with animist and Confucian beliefs blended into their religion, the refugee movements that occurred after the 1954 partition of Vietnam deeply transformed their culture. When Ngo Dinh Diem took office as premier in 1954 (and then president in 1955), he was faced with the huge problem of resettling some 860,000 refugees from North Vietnam. About 600,000 of these were Vietnamese Catholics. Most of them were former military dependents and bureaucrats with the French. American psyops (psychological operations) teams had encouraged the southward flight of these Catholics by spreading such slogans as "Christ has gone to the South," and the US Seventh Fleet had helped the French to transport the refugees. Diem, himself a Catholic, settled most of these refugees in rings of communities around Saigon and nearby cities, thereby hoping to create perimeters of loyal people. During Diem's regime the Catholics got the best of everything from the government, a policy that angered the country's Buddhist majority.

From 1954 through 1956, Diem and his American advisors used the so-called Philippine Model to try to consolidate the power of his government. The Philippine Model was based on Magsaysay's victory over the Huk movement in the Philippines. In essence it called for cadre programs to bring the government closer to the villagers, for full amnesty for guerrillas who surrendered, and for vigorous pursuit of guerrillas who continued fighting. An early Civil Affairs program, in which cadres were sent to villages to "eat, sleep, and work" with the people, was frustrated by other government bureaucracies. In 1957 it was made into a paramilitary force for Diem's powerful brother Ngo Dinh Nhu.

Elements of the Philippine Model lingered in the form of such efforts as the CIA-financed Revolutionary Development Cadres and the Open Arms amnesty program. After 1956, however, the American effort turned to developing a conventional military force. It soon became clear that the Americans were thinking in terms of a Korean Model, which would prepare for a massive enemy invasion across the 17th Parallel. The Korean Model lives on, written on the land in the form of the "McNamara Line," a bulldozed, defoliated, and sensor-seeded gash across Vietnam just below the Demilitarized Zone. Indeed, the Korean experience is largely behind reliance on military activity as a solution to the Vietnam "problem." But it was the Vietnamese leaders, particularly Nhu, who realized in the late fifties that a conventional military approach could not defeat the rebels in South Vietnam.

Early in 1959 the South Vietnamese Government began forcefully relocating villages along strategic highways. During 1961, acting without initial American advice or funds, Nhu launched the Strategic Hamlet Program. Sir Robert Thompson, the former defense minister of British Malaya, arrived with a British advisory mission, which stayed until the fall of 1965. By the summer of 1963, the South Vietnamese Government claimed to have moved two-thirds of the people of South Vietnam into strategic hamlets.

Nhu's Strategic Hamlet Program was a mixture of his own concepts of village solidarity and self-defense with the Malayan Model of counterinsurgency. The British had defeated communist rebels in Malaya by moving the population to tightly-defended centers and by severing the guerrillas' contact with people and supplies. The Strategic Hamlet Program in South Vietnam involved the compulsory relocation of all homes inside a tight village perimeter, the construction of village defenses, the control of the movement of people, and the raising of a village militia. This program was resisted by the villagers, who are economically and religiously tied to their land. It was particularly offensive to Mekong-delta villagers, who generally build their houses strung out along canals, and had to relocate their homes in hamlet clusters.

South Vietnam proved to be unlike the Philippines, Korea, and British Malaya. For example, the rebels in British Malaya had been mostly members of an identifiable ethnic minority group (Chinese). They had operated in a foodless jungle region, among tin and rubber workers who could be relocated without serious economic effects. In contrast, most NLF members are ethnically Vietnamese. They operate among agricultural people and have good supply lines. Consequently, the creation of strategic hamlets separates the people, not the guerrillas, from the food supply.

Diem and Nhu were overthrown and executed in 1963. A closet comedy of Saigon coups and intrigues ensued, while the

NLF made rapid gains in the countryside. American advisers flocked to Vietnam and pacification programs blossomed. Nevertheless, by early 1965 it was clear that the NLF was about to win. The US Air Force then began bombing North Vietnam. And when the first U.S. Marines combat unit charged up the beaches of Da Nang in March 1965 (to be met by flower-bearing Vietnamese belles!), the South Vietnam counterinsurgency effort entered a new phase. It had no name, but it could have been called either Malaya-Gone-Mad or the Devastation Model.

The nature of American methods of fighting in South Vietnam are drearily familiar to anyone tuned into the mass media. In 1969, at the peak of its activities there, the American military machine fielded more than half a million men. These men were using, or being used by, weapons systems of incredible complexity and destructive power. The NLF, rather than submitting to this onslaught, fought with redoubled determination. The North Vietnamese army (NVA), which prior to 1965 had sent few regular troops to South Vietnam, soon dispatched divisions to fight in the South.

In the face of this resistance, which the White House and Pentagon certainly had not expected, securing the countryside against the communists demanded troops in great number and with iron resolve. Such troops were not available. On the other hand, the population centers of South Vietnam were logistically susceptible to military-government control. So American military might was, and continues to be, deployed against the people of the countryside—indeed, against the countryside itself.

Search-and-destroy operations cause the forced movement of people to urban centers. The establishment of so-called free-strike zones, which are designated areas where anything moving is fair game for passing troops and aircraft, drives villagers into population concentrations. The harassment-and-interdiction (H&I) artillery rounds, which thud quite randomly every night around the cities and towns of South Vietnam, encourage people to live inside the ring of fire. Then there are the nighttime "squirrel hunts" and "turkey shoots" by Huey choppers (helicopters) looking for human game in free-strike zones; the "hosing" of targets by "spooky birds," which are C–47 aircraft that can lay down 300 rounds per second from their .50 caliber Gatling guns; and the "accidental" defoliation and deliberate chemical destruction of crops in remote areas. These and other tactics make much of rural South Vietnam hazardous to live in.

As a result of American strategy in Vietnam, and the National Liberation Front–North Vietnamese Army (NLF-NVA) resistance to that strategy, *more than one-third* of the people of South Vietnam became refugees between 1964 and 1970. Refugees continue to be "generated": in the first six months of 1970, half a million refugees were added to the official rolls. But these statistics fail to indicate the true extent of recent population movement in South Vietnam, because many people have fled in search of safety without ever passing through the US-GVN refugee-processing system. The 1970 staff report of the US Senate Refugee Subcommittee observed: "Indeed, it would appear that the greatest success achieved in the Vietnam refugee program this past year was the reclassification campaign, which, in effect, 'solved' the refugee problem by reclassifying refugees out of existence."

At present, most of the people of South Vietnam are jammed into provincial and district towns, and especially into the cities, which have grown accordingly. In 1968 it was estimated that 6,800,000 of the country's 17,200,000 inhabitants then lived in cities with populations of 20,000 or more. The wartime population growth of South Vietnamese cities is demonstrated by the following estimates: Qui Nhon, from 40,000 to 140,000; Da Nang, from 25,000 to 300,000; An Khe, from 2,000 in 1964 to 28,000 in 1968. Saigon, which was a seedy fishing village when the French took it in the nineteenth century, had a population in 1962 of 1,400,000. By 1968 there were about 4,000,000 people living in the Saigon metropolitan area.

Dr. John A. Hannah, Administrator of the Agency for International Development (AID), told the Senate Refugee Subcommittee in 1969 that he saw signs of positive change and program success in Vietnam. He focused on Operation Russell Beach as an example of positive tactical change. He cited refugee villages in the Cam Ranh Bay area as evidence of successful refugee resettlement. We may begin an examination of the "new" South Vietnam with the cases selected by Dr. Hannah.

"In an effort to minimize the number of deaths and injuries to civilians as a result of military operations," testified Dr. Hannah, "a special effort has been made to remove civilians from areas of expected conflict." Operation Russell Beach was a pilot cordon-and-sweep mission, of a type that Dr. Hannah suggested was replacing the distasteful search-and-destroy tactics. Local Vietnamese and American authorities were notified of the operation one month in advance, which, as anyone who has worked in Vietnam knows, thereby assured that the NLF also knew. On January 23, 1969 a covey of choppers descended upon the Batangan Peninsula, which lies east of Quang Ngai in the northern part of the I Corps region. They flew 12,000 people to a tent city, where GVN interrogators attempted to "separate out" NLF supporters. Meanwhile, a military operation swept the peninsula, in the course of which some hundreds of KIAs (people killed in action) were claimed and all structures were leveled.

One month after Operation Russell Beach, a Refugee Subcommittee investigator found that all the people of the peninsula had been resettled in newly-built villages a few kilometers from their former homes. All had received their resettlement payments. "The houses," observed the investigator, "are of poor quality, cramped together. Most all palm trees destroyed by gunfire . . . security is poor with curfew at nightfall." The people were being protected by three Combined Action Platoon (CAP) teams of 13 U.S. marines and 25 Popular Force troops each, two Regional Force companies of 100 men each, ten Revolutionary Development teams of 20 men each, 400 Americal Division troops, and 400 ARVN soldiers. That works out to about one soldier for every ten people. Some months later another Refugee Subcommittee investigator found that the people "understandably evidence little enthusiasm about their new surroundings," but were warned by their defenders not to return to their former homes.

Turning to the Cam Ranh Bay area resettlement success story, Dr. Hannah reported on visits to the resettlement hamlets of My Ca and Vinh Cam. The people all had stout new houses, and all able-bodied adults were employed by the Americans at Cam Ranh Base. A Refugee Subcommittee investigator added that family income in the Cam Ranh Bay area resettlement hamlets was very high by Vietnamese standards, and that nobody was farming or fishing because everybody was working for the Americans. "These are two examples of good resettlement hamlets," said Dr. Hannah.

In 1968, I drove along a superhighway through the area, past tracts of plywood houses. With me was an International Voluntary Services (IVS) volunteer who had worked there. He told me that private contractors had built whole towns there at great expense, but with profit margins written into the contracts. Village chiefs from insecure areas, particularly in the I Corps region, had been flown down and urged to bring their villages to the Cam Ranh Bay area. The US Government had obtained a 99-year lease on Cam Ranh Base, so the Vietnamese were invited to provide services for the Americans. But the program had soured, I was informed, when it was found that the area lay upon a brackish sludge unsuitable for either farming or drinking.

The fiery urbanization of the South Vietnamese people has wrenched them loose from their natural environment, as well as from the culture that psychologically linked them in harmony with their villages. In place of a Buddhist-Confucian-animist rice culture, they now have an urbanized, American-sustained war culture. Before examining the new South Vietnamese culture it is appropriate to look at the refugee-generating process in Laos and Cambodia, for it seems that many influential Americans can look at the war-bred urbanization of South Vietnam and see incipient victory. Indeed, they can see a model—a Devastation Model as I have called it—to be applied against rebels throughout the world.

Samuel P. Huntington, Chairman of the Department of

Government at Harvard University, wrote in the July 1968 issue of *Foreign Affairs*:

> In an absent-minded way the United States in Viet Nam may well have stumbled upon the answer to "wars of national liberation." The effective response lies neither in the quest for conventional military victory nor in the esoteric doctrines and gimmicks of counter-insurgency warfare. It is instead forced-draft urbanization and modernization which rapidly brings the country in question out of the phase in which a rural revolutionary movement can hope to generate sufficient strength to come to power.
>
> Time in South Viet Nam is increasingly on the side of the Government. But in the short run, with half the population still in the countryside, the Viet Cong will remain a powerful force which cannot be dislodged from its constituency so long as the constituency continues to exist.

Laos: The Subterranean Environment

Early in the nineteenth century, Meo tribesmen began pouring into what is now North Vietnam in search of fresh land to replace the wastes created by their swidden-farming in Yünnan province of southern China. Driving southward, the Meos pushed other tribes from the land, but were stopped at the edge of the Red River delta by Vietnamese armies. Their southern thrust was diverted westward into Laos. In the twentieth century, Meos also began settling in the hills of northwestern Thailand.

Of rebellious nature, the Meos of Xieng Khouang province, in northern Laos, were disarmed by the French in 1919 after a two-year war. The French also tried to force them to replant land being destroyed by their swidden-farming practices. So the Meos rearmed themselves and continued southward, only to be greeted by their new neighbors like a plague of locusts.

The Meos, or Miaos, constitute one of the few truly nomadic tribes of Indochina. Organized into fierce clans under the leadership of sorcerer-kings, they make their own muskets and are masters of small-unit warfare. About 2,500,000 Meos remain in southern China, where, in their mountain fastness, they continually breathe life into the Meo history of resistance to lowland-Chinese acculturation.

According to 1960 estimates, there are about 400,000 Meos in Laos and at least 45,000 in northwestern Thailand. Their chief cash crop is opium. In Southeast Asia, opium can be grown only at elevations above 3,000 feet. On well-developed soils covering the western slopes of hills, a field of opium—often interplanted with corn (maize)—can produce crops for ten or more consecutive seasons. Less favorably placed fields give out in two years or less. When local land is exhausted, opium-farming Meos move on to slash, burn, and cultivate fresh plots.

In 1961, a retired Indiana farmer, Edgar "Pop" Buell, got together with a former Meo sergeant in the French army, Vang Pao, to organize and supply a Meo army in northern Laos. With military supplies donated by the Department of Defense and CIA, food from AID, and transportation provided by the quasi-private Air America, "Pop" and Pao created what came to be called the Clandestine Army. This force of Meos and other tribesmen lived with their families on isolated hill-sites behind Pathet Lao (PL) lines, subsisting on airdrops and waging guerrilla war against the communists.

Meanwhile, in the Laotian capital of Vientiane, a political slapstick worthy of the wit of Graham Greene was being played out by Laotian feudatories and American bureaucracies. By 1968, Laos had a paper coalition government: the Mekong River valley was substantially under the control of the US-backed Royal Laotian Government (RLG) and the rest of the mountainous country was held by the Pathet Lao. For some years the PL had been overrunning certain northern areas in the dry season and the RLG troops, together with Vang Pao's army, had been retaking those areas during the wet season. The Clandestine Army did most of the actual fighting, while the RLG troops pulled so-called static-defense duty in lowland towns. It was a quiet little monsoon of a war, quite in keeping with the lackadaisical air of Laos.

On March 11, 1968, the communists took Phou Pha Thi, a US-Meo radar station used to guide bombing raids on North Vietnam. The Pathet Lao and North Vietnamese then pushed southward to territories they had previously left alone. In the subsequent wet-season campaign, Vang Pao's army drove farther north than had been its custom. The pendulum war was over.

Until 1968, nearly all the "refugees" in Laos had actually been dependents of Vang Pao's forces. These people moved back and forth with the cycle of fighting, living on American aid. It is estimated that on long marches, roughly one person out of every family of five died. The Refugee Subcommittee staff estimated that by 1970, owing to recurrent movement and the ravages of war, between 40 and 50 percent of the male Meos in Laos were dead and about 25 percent of the Meo women and children had also perished. "Pop" Buell summed up his ten-year career with the Meos: "It's all been running and dying, running and dying."

However, not all Laotian Meos have joined with Vang Pao. Jacques Decornoy, a *Le Monde* reporter who visited Pathet Lao areas near North Vietnam in 1968, judged that only a minority of mountain tribesmen followed the Clandestine Army. "Pop" Buell estimated that less than 10 percent of the Meos of Laos stayed to live with the Pathet Lao, but the figure may be much higher.

The Western Autonomous Zone of North Vietnam contains many Meos, some of whom must be among the North Vietnamese troops aiding the PL in Laos. In addition, since Meos have been moving southward from Laos, there are now about 250,000 Meos in northern Thailand. Thailand Meos form the core of a 1,000-man guerrilla force armed by China. These guerrillas are fighting in Thailand for the same things the US-supported Meos want in Laos: independence, land, and the right to grow and sell opium. But in Thailand, the US is helping the Thai Government to crush the Meo rebellion and to move lowland Thais into the hills.

For the Meos and others living in the Pathet Lao zone of Laos, the most striking environmental feature is a saturating deluge of bombs. The bombing of Laos escalated in four phases. The first phase, from May 1964 to October 1966, involved Laotian T-28s bombing PL troop concentrations. The second phase, running until early 1968, included American aircraft striking PL-held villages. Nineteen days after the Phou Pha Thi guidance-radar site was overrun in March 1968, President Johnson declared a halt to air strikes above the 19th Parallel in North Vietnam. At that time the bombing of Laos entered a third phase, with American jets regularly attacking the towns and villages of northern Laos.

Early in 1969, following the total halt of air strikes on North Vietnam, the fourth and continuing phase of bombing began. Fred Branfman, a former IVS volunteer, interviewed refugees from the Pathet Lao zone. "They say," he reported, "that everything was fired on, buffaloes, cows, ricefields, schools, temples, tiny shelters outside the village, in addition to, of course, all people." On some days in 1969, 800 sorties were flown, dropping napalm, phosphorous, and antipersonnel bombs. One old man described the effects of what he called fire bombs: "First the houses and fruit trees were burned, then the fields and the hillside and even the stream was on fire."

The refugees told Branfman that the Pathet Lao stayed in the forest to avoid being hit by bombs and that village youth increasingly joined the PL as the bombing intensified. The people who remained in villages lived a life described for Branfman in 1969 by refugees from the Plain of Jars, a fertile plateau in northern Laos:

> From 1965–67 they could farm but after January 1968 the planes were so many that they could only farm at night. Bombing became so intensive after January 1969 that they could hardly farm at all, bombing went on for 24 hours a day, day and night.
>
> People would run out of trenches, then run back at the sound of planes. They used to bomb first in one place, then another—but then saturation bombing began. Planes—L-21, L-19, F-105, F-86, T-28—no B-52s. Pathet Lao told them the names of the planes, that's how they knew them. . . . 1969—all planes came low, no anti-aircraft fire. They were so afraid of airplanes they had to stop

growing food. Ate 2 times a day, but after 1967 didn't eat overly much because they were afraid to burn firewood too much.

In 1960 the Plain of Jars area was the home of about 150,000 people. Early in 1970, as a vigorous Pathet Lao dry-season offensive was in progress, Vang Pao's Meos forcibly evacuated about 90,000 villagers from the Plain of Jars. Now the plateau is almost uninhabited, with its Meos and other mountain tribesmen living in refugee camps near Clandestine Army headquarters and its ethnic Lao inhabitants resettled near Vientiane. But about half of the ethnic Lao on the plain chose to flee deeper into the Pathet Lao zone.

Following the US invasion of Cambodia, the North Vietnamese and their allies took both Attopeu and Saravane in southern Laos. They then had control of the core of Indochina, the mountainous region where South Vietnam, Cambodia, and Laos meet. Many refugees fled the bombing and ground-troop action that ensued. By the fall of 1970, there were about 300,000 refugees *on official rolls* in Laos, out of a total population of 3,000,000. For their care for one year, as the Refugee Subcommittee staff pointed out, the American government has been spending the monetary equivalent of six days of bombing Laos.

There are two distinct cultures emerging in Laos, both of which are being shaped by the Americans. One is epitomized by Vientiane, which I visited in April 1969. Vientiane wallows languorously in the muds of tropic corruption. The Royal Laotian Government does not bother to collect taxes. Instead, it receives direct aid from the US, picks up a duty on gold passing through Vientiane to be smuggled to Saigon and elsewhere, or simply prints *kip*, which the US guarantees will be exchanged at the rate of 500 *kip* per dollar. Nor does the Royal Laotian Government's influence extend far from the major cities. Energetic Americans are allowed to administer their aid program right down to the recipient and to sneak about forming tribal armies to be chewed up by the war.

The crushing taut frenzy of Saigon is lacking. In South Vietnam the foreigner first learns the Vietnamese salutation, which means, "You are strong and clever, I presume?" In Laos the foreigner learns *bo pin yang*, meaning "never mind" or "who cares?" American families lounge around the American Community Association pool, forming a tight little air-conditioned Kiplingesque outpost. The kids and younger American counterinsurgents cruise downtown, buying cheap and potent Laotian marijuana. By night the Laotian government nabobs can be found at their leisure on Dong Palaine, the bar-brothel strip, protected from hazard by RLG troop units.

It is a dependent society, with the American presence preserving and even increasing feudal privilege and tribal fragmentation. Its spirit is fractured, caught in suspended animation, waiting for the Americans to relinquish their hold and move on.

The deluge of bombs saturates the countryside, and the Pathet Lao use it to fashion a second Laotian culture. Refugees describe making tools out of metallic debris; they speak of defusing cluster bomblets and creating paraffin lamps. Older refugees complain that their traditions were transformed by PL social organizations, that they were forced to do porterage. Many of their young stayed behind, however, to enjoy the stark independence of the subterranean world.

In the caves of Sam Neua Province, Jacques Decornoy found a living government. He saw small factories producing farm implements from unexploded bombs. Classes were held on the techniques of farming crater-pocked fields by night. Political education, he found, was less strident than in North Vietnam. The traditional dances of Laos were blended with nationalist and resistance themes.

Decornoy believed he was witnessing an exaltation of Laotian nationalism. Laos, however, has never been a nation. It has been a collection of disparate tribes scattered in inaccessible mountain areas, with the ethnic Lao of the lowlands forming less than 50 percent of the population. What Decornoy described was the fiery *creation* of a unified nation, being drawn together by opposition to America and her bombs. These people are not humanoids, to be enthralled by Professor Huntington's "forced-draft urbanization." They use the devastation of technological war to temper the blade of their power.

Cambodia: FARK versus FUNK

Perhaps they felt left out, becalmed in the eye of the American hurricane whipping through Thailand, Laos, and South Vietnam. Prince Sihanouk lived in pomp and dazzle, amusing the peasants with love movies in which his ministers were forced to play bit parts. On March 18, 1970, Lon Nol, the general, and Sirik Matak, the bureaucrat, took advantage of Sihanouk's absence and organized the Cambodian National Assembly to vote him out of power. With blind eagerness, Cambodia then plunged into the Indochina war.

Genuine problems preceded Sihanouk's ouster. Economic stagnation was accompanied by gnawing insurgencies. In the mountains of northeastern Cambodia, Halang and Jarai tribesmen (collectively termed the Khmer Loeu, although many Jarai are South Vietnamese Montagnards) were in rebellion under the guidance of NLF cadres. The Khmer Loeu war was following a familiar pattern. Beginning in 1959, the Cambodian Government had moved 25,000 lowlanders into the mountains to clear the forest and create a rubber plantation. In May 1968 most of the 60,000 swidden-farming Khmer Loeu deserted their villages for the mountain fastness. There, with the help of the NLF, they organized a 1,200-man independence army. The Cambodian Army (Forces Armées Royales Khmers, or FARK) were fighting the Khmer Loeu with poor men's search-and-destroy operations, to little success.

FARK was having even more trouble with the Khmer Rouge, a group of lowland rebels. About 3,000 Khmer Rouge had been armed by the NLF and Peking-oriented Cambodians of Chinese origin. On the South Vietnam border, the Khmer Rouge were fighting alongside the NVA-NLF forces. In western Cambodia, the Khmer Rouge were apparently an independent force led by the brilliant intellectual Hou Youn, who had been exiled from Pnom Penh in 1967. To deal with these rebellions and with the NVA-NLF soldiers in Cambodia, Sihanouk had been making friendly moves toward Western powers. Most of Lon Nol's 35,000 FARK troops were tied to outposts, being attacked occasionally by roving bands of Khmer Rouge and Khmer Loeu.

These problems were as nothing compared to what followed Sihanouk's removal. The present chaos of Cambodia is burning testimony to Sihanouk's cavalier diplomatic genius, to his personal ability in peacefully suppressing strong forces. The first ghost to be loosed was the ancient enmity between the Khmers and Vietnamese.

The French had brought some Vietnamese to Cambodia as colonial administrators and rubber-plantation workers, and had allowed others to migrate there. Cambodia's ethnic Vietnamese population grew to about 400,000. A large proportion of the country's technicians and artisans were Vietnamese. Furthermore, control of Cambodia's trade was mostly in the hands of the ethnic Chinese and the ethnic Vietnamese.

Unlike the two Vietnams, Cambodia can be considered underpopulated. Its approximately seven million inhabitants live in an area that covers almost 70,000 square miles, about 80 percent of which are arable. So when Sihanouk let 60,000 Vietnamese settle in areas along the South Vietnamese border, the Cambodian peasants, being Therevada Buddhists and not customarily warlike, generally moved over as the more aggressive Vietnamese moved in.

Seeking to whip up anti-Vietnamese hatred, Lon Nol organized a "riot" in Pnom Penh. A mob composed of bureaucrats, students, and soldiers in plainclothes sacked the North Vietnamese and NLF embassies a few days prior to the removal of Sihanouk. FARK's first operation after Lon Nol's take-over was the internment of almost all Vietnamese in Cambodia and the massacre of hundreds of Vietnamese. These internments and slaughters were, by all accounts, the work of the army acting without Cambodian peasant support. In fact, shortly after the coup, FARK shot a number of unarmed Cambodian demonstrators who were pro-Sihanouk.

Meanwhile, in South Vietnam, intense pressure was being put on President Thieu to invade Cambodia and put an end to the massacre of Vietnamese. Late in April 1970, ARVN and US forces launched an armored and airborne assault across the border, ostensibly to clear NVA-NLF sanctuaries in Cambodia. Some 50,000 Vietnamese fled Cambodia's border provinces for the relative safety of South Vietnam. Shortly thereafter, 150,000 more Vietnamese were evacuated by armed flotilla down the Mekong River from Pnom Penh to Saigon. It was a bizarre spectacle even for Indochina: one army was rescuing its ethnic brothers from the wrath of its "ally." Most of the 200,000 ethnic Vietnamese remaining in Cambodia were kept in provincial detention centers.

By late 1970, the Cambodian war, which rapidly spread throughout the country after Sihanouk's removal, had made refugees of about one million Khmers, or ethnic Cambodians. These people crowded into the provincial capitals, and into Pnom Penh. Pnom Penh swiftly became "Saigonized." Early in 1970, Cambodia's capital contained 250,000 ethnic Vietnamese, 250,000 ethnic Chinese, and 150,000 Khmers. Within a year, the Vietnamese had either gone or been imprisoned, Khmers had occupied their former houses, and the city's population had doubled.

Changes in Cambodia occur with an amphetamine rush. The years of war that have transformed Laos and South Vietnam are compressed into days and even hours. People are mashed into urban centers. South Vietnamese and American bombers range over the countryside. By the fall of 1970 the economy was paralyzed. The export of rice and rubber, Cambodia's export mainstays, had ceased. Foreign currency reserves were low and the government was printing about $10 million worth of currency per month. Over three-fourths of the country was insecure. Transportation was intermittent. FARK troops were billeted in a new tourist hotel at Siem Reap and Angkor was the new sanctuary for communist forces.

Lon Nol's army has grown to about 140,000 men. His government has declared Cambodia a republic, thereby taking the "Royales" out of FARK. This republic clearly will not survive without massive dollar transfusions. The US swiftly gave Cambodia $8.9 million and pledged $40 million in military aid for 1971. In December 1970, Congress approved $255 million in aid for Cambodia. This bill included $70 million in economic aid, although economists predict that Cambodia needs $230 million in such aid for 1971, and twice that amount for 1972.

Lon Nol's efforts to unite Cambodians in a nationalist, anti-communist, anti-Vietnamese crusade have been complicated by the interminable presence of his South Vietnamese "allies." The South Vietnamese Government has not officially recognized Cambodia's borders, although the NLF has. About 15,000 ARVN troops have remained in occupation of border areas. They have also established a "mini-Cam Ranh base" at Neak Leong, on the Mekong River near Pnom Penh. American-made black-market goods pour out of Neak Leong. The ARVN forces use massive firepower wherever they operate. In general, the South Vietnamese appear as players of the American role in the Cambodian theater. By November 1970 the fields had dried out sufficiently for a 6,000-man ARVN unit to race about Cambodia's eastern provinces, laying waste to the countryside in a vain search for the NVA.

An estimated 30,000 Thai troops have massed on Cambodia's western border, and at least three battalions of them are being specifically trained for fighting in Cambodia. The Thais have never officially recognized Cambodia's border and may well desire the Cambodian border provinces that the French forced them to cede in the nineteenth century. With the help of the Japanese, the Thais took these provinces again during the early 1940s, but were forced to return them to the French after World War II. By late 1970, Thai troops were patrolling both sides of the border, and apparently were holding out for more US aid before plunging into the Cambodian fray.

Political conditions in the Cambodian countryside are obscure. With the backing of Peking and Hanoi, Prince Sihanouk is apparently striving to rally the various rebel forces in Cambodia—Khmer Rouge, Khmer Loeu, and NLF—into a single force called FUNK (Front Uni National Kampuchea). Vigorous political organization of the Khmer peasantry by the NLF began shortly after Sihanouk's ouster. Richard Dudman, who was captured and released by FUNK, wrote an account similar to Decornoy's report from the Pathet Lao zone: "we felt we were watching the terrorization of the peasants of Cambodia . . . we were observing the welding together of the local population with the guerrillas. The peasants were turning to the fighters as their best friends."

It is too early to say what will happen to Cambodia, other than that the future augurs continuing war and destruction. Both the South Vietnamese and the Thais may—with US backing—carve border provinces from Cambodia. Lon Nol and FAK may hold out in Pnom Penh and the provincial capitals of central Cambodia, also with US support. In the Cambodian countryside, FUNK may be able to weld together a genuine rural revolution, tempered by the application of American-supplied weaponry.

Saigon: Fractured Spirit

Saigon glints with dull metallic sheen beneath clinging exhaust clouds. By day its arteries are hypertense with motorcycle traffic, as people rush with set faces. At night its streets clear, sirens scream, choppers slap overhead, and taut guards wait in squat bunkers. Garbage lies uncollected, public works decay, and each man seeks to advance the fortune of his family. Saigon is a war-dependent, totalitarian metropolis, where people are cut off from one another and from their natural environment. It is probably the most unstable, explosive urban system on the planet.

What passes for civil order in Saigon is bought by the Americans and South Vietnamese Government with their two chief commodities: terror and affluence. It was terror in the countryside—the application of the Devastation Model—that drove many of Saigon's four million inhabitants to the city, and it is terror that keeps them there. Two-thirds of Saigon's meager municipal budget ($8.7 million in 1966) goes to salaries for officials and police. Nets of national police, military police, secret police, faction enforcers, and crypto-agents entwine the society. The jails of South Vietnam are jammed with thousands of political prisoners: 30,000 according to the chief US public-safety adviser, 50,000 according to a South Vietnamese Senate committee; or 100,000 by the reckoning of Don Luce, a World Council of Churches observer. All prisoners expect exotic torture. Many get it.

The ultimate in terror was demonstrated in Saigon and other South Vietnamese cities during Tet 1968. Towns and sections of cities were taken by the North Vietnamese Army and National Liberation Front. Whatever the communists held was exploded into dust by the Americans and South Vietnamese. Therefore, by logic simple and brutal, the communists could not hold a city. I saw local residents react to this demonstration of power by forming block self-defense units to keep communists and the consequent rain of fire from overwhelming their homes.

The national mobilization that followed Tet 1968 was designed to enlist every able-bodied South Vietnamese in the army "for the duration." This universal conscription is a means of control as well as a source of manpower. ARVN can watch a man, inculcate him with its view of the world, and cause him to take up arms against the NLF. Early in 1965, a relatively small part of the population was directly involved in the war. By the end of 1968, almost everyone in South Vietnam had been forced into the struggle.

Along with terror, the GVN buys compliance with the sickly-sweet affluence that has come with American war. Professor Huntington, by way of documenting the success of forced-draft urbanization, cited a study of the Saigon slum known as Xom Chua. Early in 1965, 33 percent of the adult males of Xom Chua were unemployed. Eighteen months later, the slum's population had increased 30 percent, unemployment had fallen to 5 percent, and average income had doubled. This economic boom extended to the rural areas where

I worked. By 1970, there were about one-third more consumer goods in South Vietnam than there had been in 1965.

What precipitated this miraculous glut? The population was drained from productive tasks in order to staff and service the fourth-largest army in the world, and the war destroyed much of the infrastructure of South Vietnam's economy. It has become an import-reliant economy, needing constant injections of dollars or other hard foreign exchange to keep it alive. These injections come from the US Government.

South Vietnam's primary dollar source is US military spending, which, despite troop withdrawals, put an estimated $350 million into the economy during 1970. In the same year $354 million in direct military aid was given to the ARVN. The GVN received about $170 million in development-project aid during 1970, as well as surplus agricultural commodities valued at $105 million.

The United States also supplies dollars to the GVN under the commercial import program. Licensed importers buy these dollars ($240 million in 1970) at 118 piasters per dollar. This is the program that has filled South Vietnam with luxury imports, such as flashy scooters and transistorized devices. And with piasters selling at black-market rates of over 400 to the dollar, the program has filled a lot of government and business pockets as well.

This gush of dollars presents an opportunity for a saturnalia of corruption at the American taxpayers' expense, an opportunity that neither Vietnamese nor Americans have let pass. The action is fast and rich in Saigon, involving as it does the "shadow community" of American deserters and con men, the "ghosts" on GVN payrolls, the currency manipulators, the post exchange (PX) "channel operators," and outright dockside thieves. The squeeze runs all the way from the GI who moves PX Salems through his girlfriend to three of Thieu's four top generals, who have been exposed for their involvement in a massive currency-smuggling ring.

Corruption in Saigon shades into virtue and becomes the highest virtue of increasing family wealth. To most government employees, whose incomes are paltry, corruption is necessity. Nevertheless, there is something corrupting, and demeaning in the whole fabric of a society that distorts itself in order to hook onto the American dollar-flow.

This economy of American junk is now suffering the pangs of troop withdrawal. With money in circulation increasing about 30 percent per year and foreign currency reserves falling steadily, the GVN has had to find a new income source. President Thieu has lacked the temerity to increase domestic taxes. Most GVN income is derived from various import duties, which represent taxes on American-financed imports. In October 1969, over the objection of the National Assembly, Thieu slapped a heavy, so-called austerity tax on imports. The price of gasoline doubled, thereby increasing the price of rice and other necessities requiring transportation. From 1965 through 1969, inflation had cruised along at an average increase of 27 percent per year. In the first seven months of 1970, owing to American troop withdrawals and the austerity tax, prices in Saigon rose 22 percent.

As affluence decreases, the Thieu government must dispense increasing terror. The torture of Saigon student leaders galvanized student demonstrations in the spring of 1970. Soon disabled veterans hit the streets to demand increased benefits. Veterans of Special Forces units, such as Mike Force and the Civilian Irregular Defense Groups, spearheaded the riots, because these particular veterans are not entitled to any disability benefits; a fully-disabled Special Forces hireling receives only $200 worth of piasters and a discharge. Militant Buddhists joined the rioters. The government responded by shutting down the schools in the Saigon area and repressing demonstrations, first with tear gas and later with bullets.

This riot-repression-riot cycle is the sign of the future. In 1970, although the flow of dollars had scarcely begun to ebb, the imminent crash already could be felt. The GVN devalued the piaster from 118 to 275 per dollar in October, even though the new rate does not apply to most of the lucrative commercial import racket.

The black carnival is coming to an end, and the people of Saigon know it. The process of American withdrawal is being felt by the 140,000 Saigon citizens directly employed by Americans; the hundreds of thousands of whores, some 30,000 of whom ply their trade in Saigon; the thousands of Saigon "cowboys"—the juveniles who hustle a life from the shabby-gaudy Saigon night; and the unguessed numbers of launderers, renters, suppliers, and other dependents on American war. The whole hooked human society can feel the economy coming down.

Presidents Nixon and Thieu were assured in March 1969 that the postwar development of Vietnam could proceed at an orderly pace, presuming that all governments and peoples involved would follow the plot-line laid down in the Joint Development Group report. The group, headed by Professor Vu Quoc Thuc and David E. Lillienthal, specified that for the success of their scheme, peace and stability must reign in South Vietnam. Central economic planning must be supplemented by cooperation in the private sector. Furthermore, they wrote, "Development will not occur unless the mass of the people of Vietnam understand what it is for, embrace its objectives, accept the sacrifices it implies, and strive to bring it about."

If the people of South Vietnam could be shunted about by the recommendations of US-GVN committees, reality would be a prosperous print-out. But the South Vietnamese are humans, not humanoids. Their family structures have been torn asunder. The war has plucked the people from their villages, from the sources of their identity and strength. It has fractured their shared symbols and has assaulted their minds with the violence and materialism of American war. Robert Jay Lifton has defined the common attitudes South Vietnamese take toward their obsession, Americans: dependency, coupled with antagonism.

"The people's confidence is now frozen, their hope has now disappeared," wrote South Vietnamese Senator Thai Lang Nghiem in 1970. Senator Nghiem continued:

> The heart of the matter is not the offensive of the Communists but the dirty nature of our own people, our own

leaders. Our minds are dirty, our hearts are dirty. It is clear that we are up to our necks in corruption. It has entered our bloodstream, our lungs, our hearts. It is no longer an individual disease. It is systematized. It has got hold of the whole regime. Corruption comes from the organization of power. To stamp out corruption means to reorganize power—in this case, political power, political institutions. Power must be put back in the hands of the people. The New Year of the Dog is the New Year of general fatigue, of a feeling of pain after being beaten up.

Professor Ly Chanh Trung, a leading Catholic intellectual, told a Saigon University audience in 1968:

Being a Vietnamese, I can no longer put up with the sight of foreigners who presume to have the right to destroy my country, with the most modern and terrible means, and all in the name of "protecting the freedom" of the people of southern Viet Nam—that is to say, a kind of "freedom" which the inhabitants of the southern part of Viet Nam have been throwing up and vomiting out for the last ten years already, without yet being able to swallow. . . . the only way Americans then knew to "protect freedom" was by the several millions of tons of bombs used to crush to pieces the very land of Viet Nam, and by the gigantic streams of dollars which deluge Vietnamese society in the south—that is to say, by destroying the very roots of the material and spiritual foundations of this country.

The issue of who shall govern Saigon pales before the question, "Can any power govern Saigon?" The seethe of Saigon's communal wranglings is beyond comprehension. The CIA has informed us that at least 30,000 NLF agents have infiltrated the GVN, but it is by no means certain that the communists would rapidly prevail if the United States withdrew.

There are signs that a political "third force" is coalescing around Duong Van Minh, probably the only political leader in South Vietnam who is known and admired throughout the country. Minh was in exile during the 1967 national election, but now he is back, voicing support for students and veterans and apparently preparing for the 1971 presidential campaign.

A major policy statement by his supporter, Ngo Cong Duc, appeals to attitudes shared by a broad spectrum of South Vietnamese: the desire for peace and the belief that peace can come only after the Americans leave Vietnam.

North Vietnam: Tempered Blade

The Democratic Republic of Vietnam (DRV) took full control of North Vietnam in 1954. In the words of Bernard Fall, "It inherited an area that had been ravaged twice in less than a decade: its land plundered by the Japanese and Chinese and its communications bombed by the U.S. Air Force in 1944–45; literally plowed under by French tanks and devastated by Viet-Minh saboteurs and guerrillas from 1946 until the cease-fire." Most of its technicians fled to France or South Vietnam. Its industries were nearly immobile, its agricultural land was subject to flooding and drought, and its growing population was pressing heavily on resources.

The regime set out to consolidate political control and to reform agriculture in one fell swoop. Everyone was pigeonholed into an economic class and all farmers were allotted land. These reforms only carved more finely an already fragmented landholding structure. Unlike the Mekong delta, where the French had opened new land and established a Vietnamese class of large landowners, most of the Red River delta was farmed by small landowners working their own land.

Party cadres enforced land reform with brutal zeal. During 1955–56, an estimated 50,000 recalcitrant peasants were executed and about twice as many were sent to forced-labor camps. When the farmers revolted in Nghe An, Ho Chi Minh's home province, they were swiftly suppressed by the North Vietnamese Army. In August 1956 Ho Chi Minh confessed that the party had erred in its classification of "landlords" and "rich peasants," so prisoners were released and land reform proceeded more slowly.

Distribution of land was only the first stage of reform. The second stage was the formation of cooperatives, with peasants pooling their land and working it together. Government aid went to the cooperatives and pressure was put on individual farmers by the party and various village associations. By 1961, 85 percent of the land in North Vietnam was in cooperatives and 10 percent of these cooperatives had entered the third stage of land reform—socialist cooperatives, or state-managed farms.

The face of the land had changed by the early sixties. Instead of myriad, tiny, irregular paddies, there were rectangular plots that stretched for great distances. State irrigation projects had ended flooding in many areas, which made it possible to raise and harvest two or three crops per year. Agricultural production was increasing by four percent per year.

The DRV also developed its industries. South Vietnam, although agriculturally much richer than the north, has few known industrial raw materials. In contrast, North Vietnam has large reserves of coal and iron, as well as deposits of apatite (used to make chemical fertilizer). It also has a mining complex near the Chinese border that produces wolfram (a source of tungsten), tin, and uranium. According to DRV sources, North Vietnam's industrial concerns grew in number from 41 in 1954 to 1,100 by 1964. In the same period, the DRV claimed an average annual industrial growth rate of eight percent.

From early 1965 through most of 1968, American aircraft bombed North Vietnam. Westerners who have visited North Vietnam agree that bombing targets included the transportation system (roads, railroads, bridges, and fuel-storage areas), industries, irrigation dikes, Catholic churches, schools, hospitals, whole villages, and suburban sections of the cities of Hanoi and Haiphong.

The avowed American purpose in bombing was to break the will and ability of the North Vietnamese to send men and supplies to South Vietnam. Reports from visitors to the North, and the development of the war in the South, indicate that bombing strengthened the will of the North Vietnamese and caused them to send many troops and arms to the South. (I observed this phenomenon in central Vietnam early in 1968, when NVA forces armed much better than local South Vietnamese troops were prevented by air power from exterminating us Americans.)

Bombing North Vietnam forced a shift of power from cumbersome national bureaucracies to local levels. Also, people eagerly joined government programs in the face of the immediate and obvious threat from the skies. As the chief of a village administrative committee told Gérard Chaliand, "Everything has been more straightforward since the air attacks started: labour is easier to mobilize."

Medical services were extended. As a result, all lowland and many mountain villages now have clinics, and the district and provincial towns have hospitals. Emphasis during the bombing was on swift treatment of wounds under local conditions. Village sanitation was improved with the installation of toilets and sealed wells.

Children were evacuated from cities during the bombing. They wore palm fronds for camouflage when walking outside by day. Trenches leading to stout bunkers were dug beside their school desks. Despite the evacuation, primary education became almost universal. Furthermore, university-level technical education continued throughout the period of bombing. Education has been integrated with agricultural work. National history is taught, with emphasis on Vietnamese resistance to Chinese, Mongol, Japanese, French, and American invaders. Students compile lists of American "outrages" and "people's victories."

Factories were dismantled and dispersed to caves and thatched buildings. The bombs stimulated speedy expansion of the road network, with road-building initiative shifting to local work crews. A grass-roots damage-repair system kept traffic moving at a volume higher than the pre-bombing level.

Today, many of the young village men still leave for "the front," which means either the army or construction and industry. Women work the land, staff village self-defense units, and in general have the same social roles as men. All villagers regularly drill to prepare for resistance to invasion.

While American bureaucrats mesmerize themselves with swelling body counts, the DRV is pushing a vigorous birth-

ECOLOGY OF DEVASTATION: INDOCHINA

control campaign! Population pressure is also being relieved by relocating hundreds of thousands of lowlanders on cooperative farms in the highlands. This policy is doubtless causing friction with the mountain tribes. However, as tribespeople have been integrated with the army and government since Viet Minh days, relations between the highlanders and lowlanders should be relatively peaceful.

The bombing destroyed many industrial structures and expectation of future bombing postpones construction of new factories and dams. Visitors report that Hanoi is drab, with few new buildings. The life of North Vietnam is in the countryside. Its strength is the will and unity of its people. The armed peasantry, and lack of phalanxes of guards around leaders and public buildings, are in marked contrast to South Vietnam, where Ky and Thieu normally whisk by helicopter from fortress to fortress.

Animistic religious beliefs have been more completely purged in North Vietnam than they have in the South. "As for the spirit that is supposed to watch over the village," a peasant told Gérard Chaliand, "anyone who wishes to pay homage to it is free to do so; few people bother, except the old. Since 1957 there has been no more talk of the guardian dragon objecting to wells being dug. . . ." Yet in the North new and powerful links to the village have been forged, based on progress, nationalism, and resistance.

I once saw a North Vietnamese propaganda film. People sang patriotic songs as they fashioned tools by hand. Alarms blared, tools were dropped and guns picked up, and everyone moved rapidly and calmly to duty stations. The American planes came over spewing bombs, the antiaircraft crew and rifle-wielding peasants shot into the sky. Planes fell, and pilots were led off by stern villagers. The imagery of this is incandescent: disciplined, vibrant humanity defeating gray machines of death.

The great irony of the Indochina war is that American firepower has had opposite effects on the peoples of the two Vietnams. In the South, the population and government have been concentrated in war-dependent urban clots and the spirit of

FRACTURED SPIRIT, TEMPERED BLADE

the people has been fractured by American presence. The people of the North have been driven to the countryside, made more self-reliant, brought closer to the land; their spirit has been tempered to a fine cutting strength. When the American assault upon the environment of Indochina ceases, the peoples of South Vietnam, Cambodia, and Laos will probably turn to North Vietnam and its allies as guides in the restoration of their habitats.

CHAPTER TWO

The Green Devolution

It is easy to forget, especially when eating rehydrated nutrition chips in Vietnamese mess halls, that human life depends on green plants. The chlorophyll of green plants captures solar energy and converts it, through the process of photosynthesis, into forms of chemically-bound energy that can be used by human beings and other living things. In the energy cycle of life on Earth, green plants are classified by ecologists as constituting trophic level 1, which is often termed the producer level. Trophic level 2 is composed of herbivores, which get their energy by consuming green vegetation. Trophic levels 3 and 4 are made up of carnivores, which eat herbivores or, as in the case of level 4, other carnivores. Trophic level 5 consists of decomposers, which are microorganisms capable of changing matter into forms that can be cycled through living systems.

To a counterinsurgent, plants are the allies of the insurgent. Foliage conceals the insurgent and prevents aircraft from landing. Food crops feed the insurgent. In South Vietnam, a nation that was wholly reliant on agricultural crops until it became a US dependent, the ownership of cropland is a fundamental economic and political issue used by the insurgent. And on at least two occasions during 1965 and 1966, when the American military attempted to burn all oxygen in defoliated forests by saturating them with flaming napalm, plants were used as consumers of the insurgent's oxygen and exploited as components of the insurgent's funeral pyre.

Many attempts have been made to deprive the Indochinese insurgent of his allies, the plants. Forests have been inundated with defoliating chemicals. Crops have been covered with killing sprays. Rice caches have been destroyed. Landing zones have been blasted in the forests, adding to the countless craters gouged by bombs and shells directed at the insurgent himself. Huge bulldozers known as Rome plows have stripped roadsides and carved grids in jungles. And people have been driven into population concentrations, thereby taking remote land out of production and keeping tenant farmers under the influence of government-protected landlords.

The Second Indochina War is, in part, an attack on the producer level of Indochina's living-energy cycle. Herbicidal chemicals have been deployed as weapons in this attack. Two aspects of the use of herbicides in Indochina are of paramount ecological importance. First, very little is known about the environmental consequences of using herbicides in Indochina. Second, what little is known about herbicides indicates that they cause long-term damage not only to green plants, but also to all trophic levels of the living environment.

Late in 1967, the Midwest Research Institute produced for the Defense Department a document entitled *Assessment of Ecological Effects of Extensive or Repeated Use of Herbicides* (the MRI Report). This report noted that, "To our knowledge *no* articles or books have been addressed to the subject of long-term ecological effects of herbicides, integrated with studies of flora and fauna, rangeland, forests, other nonagricultural lands, waterways, lakes and reservoirs." The MRI Report added, "To assess the use of herbicides upon an ecosystem, we are confronted with serious knowledge deficiencies. A specific 'natural' ecosystem has not yet been completely defined in that man has not been able to analyze one in its entirety."

Most studies of ecosystems and herbicides have been carried out in temperate climates. As the MRI Report stated, "The magnitude of ecological assessment in respect to the

Vietnam bioclimate becomes evident when one considers the proportionality of the South Vietnam vegetational biomass [weight of living organisms in an ecosystem] of 600,000 lb/hectare to the England/U.S.A. average woodland plant biomass of a few thousand lb/hectare."

The dangers and confusions of the Indochina war limit field research. Inquiry is further hampered by Defense Department information control. In the summer of 1970, the Herbicide Assessment Commission of the American Association for the Advancement of Science (AAAS) went to South Vietnam to launch a study of the ecological effects of herbicides. The commission's leader, Dr. Matthew S. Meselson of Harvard University, reported, "We've been given every other kind of cooperation, but we can't get the most basic information we need—a list of areas sprayed, and when, and with what. . . . We were told the information is classified 'confidential,' though the enemy certainly knows where we sprayed." The fetus-deforming capability of 2,4,5-T, a defoliant chemical widely used in Indochina and the United States, was known and concealed by the Defense Department and other government agencies for many years (as indicated in Chapter 5). We cannot know what other secrets the Defense Department is sitting on.

The visible tip of the information iceberg indicates that herbicides do even more than kill green plants and consequently damage the herbivores, carnivores, and decomposers in the living-energy cycle. The herbicides used in Indochina also have been proven to have direct poisoning effects on certain fauna, including human beings. If someone asserts that a herbicide is "safe," his assertion is based on a wealth of ignorance; it is also based on a policy judgment of how much damage and risk will be tolerated in order to achieve the "benefits" of herbicide use.

The peoples of Indochina have close economic and psychological ties to the plants of their environments. The war prevents them from using, preserving, or restoring their forests. Their abandoned cropland is subjected to craterization, chemical application, and natural deterioration. In South Vietnam the war preserves an exploitative landlord system, which takes from farmers much of the income produced by the plants they grow. According to the Joint Development Group, the farmers of South Vietnam make up three-fourths of the country's population but receive only one-third of its national income.

A Green Revolution is sweeping the underdeveloped countries of the world. New strains of rice, wheat, and other crops are dramatically increasing agricultural production in many nations. One of these strains, popularly referred to as miracle rice, has been introduced in South Vietnam and Laos by American agriculturists. Yet South Vietnam, once a major exporter of rice, now imports American rice. What has happened is that in Indochina the Green Revolution has been overwhelmed by what can be called the Green Devolution, caused by American war. By applying destructive trigger factors to the environments of Indochina, the war reduces the quantity and diversity of green plants. Complex, life-rich ecosystems are being succeeded by environments poorer in life and more hostile to humanity. The Green Devolution is analogous to the creation of a human society in which the harsh emotions and intellect of the warrior reign supreme.

Operation Ranch Hand (Hades)

In the 1930s, chemists identified the auxins, or hormones, that regulate plant growth. The most powerful plant hormone they discovered was 2,4-dichlorophenoxyacetic acid, or 2,4-D. The chemical synthesis of 2,4-D was described in June 1941 (the original pound of synthetic 2,4-D is preserved for posterity by the Smithsonian Institution). It was observed that an overdose of 2,4-D touched off wild growth in broad-leaved plants and killed them.

E. J. Kraus of the University of Chicago wrote to a wartime chemical review committee known as the ABC Committee that it might be interested in "the toxic properties of growth-regulating substances for the destruction of crops or the limitation of crop production." In 1943, Kraus and others at the University of Chicago began testing 2,4-D on food crops, including rice. By 1944, herbicide testing was a major program at Fort Detrick, a chemical and biological warfare development center established at Frederick, Maryland, in 1942. George Merck of the ABC Committee wrote, "Only the rapid ending of the war prevented field trials in an active theatre of synthetic agents that would, without injury to human or animal life, affect the growing crops and make them useless."

Herbicides, which were originally developed as modern technology's improvement on the salts applied to the fields of Carthage, became a major means of managing vegetation in the United States. In 1950, the production of herbicides totaled 14 million pounds; in 1966, production exceeded 220 million pounds. During the 1960s, herbicides represented the fastest-growing segment of the agricultural chemical industry, with 1966 production accounting for 26 percent of the country's total chemical tonnage and 44 percent of its total chemical sales value.

Beginning early in the 1940s, researchers at Fort Detrick focused on another possible use of herbicides: as tools to destroy thick vegetation in connection with landings on Pacific islands. A chemical known as ammonium thiocyanate was ready to be used as a defoliant in June 1945, but apparently it was not used because its name sounded too much like the poison called cyanide.

Undeterred by the conclusion of World War II, Detrick researchers continued to test about 12,000 potential defoliants. By 1959 they had developed a mixture of undiluted butyl esters of 2,4-D and of its close chemical relative, 2,4,5-trichlorophenoxyacetic acid (2,4,5-T). This mixture was applied to a forest at Camp Drum, New York, where it denuded an area of four square miles.

Defoliation trials were begun in South Vietnam in July 1961 under the guidance of J. W. Brown. "Even though wartime conditions interfered with the collection of detailed data," stated the MRI Report, "these tests established that the esters of 2,4-D and 2,4,5-T were active in killing a majority of the species encountered in Vietnam, providing the herbicide spray was properly applied to the vegetation during a period of active growth."

The mixture of 2,4-D and 2,4,5-T esters became the standard Indochinese jungle defoliant called Agent Orange. Agent Orange was used interchangeably with Agent Purple (a slightly different combination of the esters of 2,4-D and 2,4,5-T), until Purple was discontinued because of its cost.

Agent White consists of 2,4-D combined with picloram, which is a herbicide that decomposes relatively slowly. According to the MRI Report, "This combination provides relatively longer duration control of a wide spectrum of woody plants, plus the advantages of accurate spray placement where volatility creates problems."

Agents Orange, Purple, and White are systemic herbicides, which act on plants by entering their internal systems. However, Agent Blue, the principal crop-destroying herbicide used in Indochina, is another type of herbicide. Composed of cacodylic acid, it is classified, according to the MRI Report, as one of the dessicants, or contact herbicides, "which injure foliage by direct chemical action on contact, causing the leaves to turn brown, curl, dry up, and wither." These four agents are the only herbicides that the Defense Department has admitted using in Indochina. (See Table 1 for the composition and uses of each of these four military herbicides.)

The rationale for using defoliants in counterinsurgency operations was succinctly stated by F. J. Delmore at the First Defoliation Conference in 1963:

> The capability of destroying cover and concealment to defend against and fight off guerrilla and other types of tactics is absolutely essential. When we clear vegetation from roadsides, railways, and canals, we substantially reduce the opportunity for ambush, and thus allow our own operations to proceed in a more timely manner. Defoliants would also be used to demarcate boundaries. Defoliation could be used to clear gun emplacements, open up fields of fire, mark areas of bombing, or test whether or not a particular area was camouflage or actual vegetation.

Table 1: Composition and Characteristics of Military Herbicides

Agent	Composition		Lb/Gal AE*	Purpose
Orange	n-Butyl ester 2,4-D	50% (wt)	4.2	General defoliation
	n-Butyl ester 2,4,5-T	50% (wt)	3.7	Forest-Brush
		Total	7.9	Broad-leaved crops
Purple	n-Butyl ester 2,4-D	50% (wt)	4.2	General defoliation
	n-Butyl ester 2,4,5-T	30% (wt)	2.2	Interim agent used inter-
	Isobutyl ester 2,4,5-T	20% (wt)	1.5	changeably with Orange
		Total	7.9	
White (Tordon 101)	Tri-isopropanolamine salt 2,4-D		2.0	Forest defoliation
	Tri-isopropanolamine salt picloram		0.54	Long-term jungle control
		Total	2.54	Brush suppression
Blue (Phyter 560-G)	Sodium cacodylate	27.7%		Rapid defoliation (short duration)
	Free cacodylic acid	4.8%		Grassy plant control
	Water; sodium chloride bal.		3.1	Rice destruction

* Active Equivalent of the acid.
Source: The MRI Report

Like other counterinsurgency programs in Indochina, the herbicide operation rapidly expanded at a rate unrelated to rational policy objectives, as if it had taken an overdose of its own growth hormones. On November 29, 1961 the Special Spray Flight of the 309th Aerial Commando Squadron, USAF, received its first adapted C-123 cargo planes. The herbicide campaign was publicly named Operation Ranch Hand, but was assigned a more appropriate code name, Operation Hades. In December 1962 it was announced in Saigon that Ranch Hand (Hades) had completed "defoliation of canals and rivers in the south and a pass south of Qui Nhon." In November of that year, the South Vietnamese Air Force had announced that it had begun spraying cropland.

From this rather modest beginning involving little more than the spraying of transportation routes and base perimeters, Ranch Hand has expanded into an operation that involves spraying herbicides on whole ecosystems in South Vietnam, Cambodia, and Laos. (Herbicides have not been used on North Vietnam.) Various agencies have issued a welter of conflicting statements concerning the extent of herbicide application. (See Table 2 for US Defense Department and NLF estimates of areas sprayed with herbicides in South Vietnam.) American scientists investigating herbicide damage in South Vietnam estimate that by the end of 1970 about one-seventh of that nation's land area had been sprayed with herbicides, and that 20 percent of its forests had been defoliated.

The MRI Report noted that the following "targets" had been hit: nipa-palm and mangrove forests along river estuaries, tropical rain forests, upland forests, foliage around villages and military posts, roadsides, the southern portion of the Demilitarized Zone, swamps and canals in the Mekong delta, and also the Sihanouk Trail in northeastern Cambodia and the Ho Chi Minh Trail in southern Laos. The report also took notice of crop destruction, adding that "relatively few details about crop destruction missions are available."

The MRI Report gives the impression that herbicides have been applied only to identifiable targets, such as NLF trails and base camps. In fact, as I have seen for myself, broad for-

Table 2: US Defense Department and NLF Estimates of Areas Sprayed with Herbicides in South Vietnam.

Year	Area Sprayed (in 1,000 hectares)* Defense Dep't.	NLF	Percentage of Total Forest Area Sprayed Defense Dep't.	NLF
1961	More than 10	More than 10	—	—
1962	More than 10	10	—	—
1963	10	320	—	3%
1964	30	500	—	5
1965	60	700	1%	7
1966	300	880	3	9
1967	600	900	5	10
1968	510	990	5	10
1969	490	1,090	5	11
1970	?	More than 420	?	More than 4
Total Annual Spraying (1961–69)	2,020	5,400	20%	55%
Total area sprayed one or more times (1961–69)	1,800	2,500	18%	25%

* One hectare = 2.471 acres.
Source: Figures presented by Arthur H. Westing to the American Association for the Advancement of Science convention, December 29, 1970.
Note: Defense figures are based on gallons of spray expended, and NLF figures are based on ground observation. The spraying of Agent Blue on crops is included only in NLF data.

ests have been covered with defoliants. American biologists have observed spray damage 30 miles from the zone of application, indicating that Defense Department estimates of wind-drift range are far too low.

The conditions under which Operation Ranch Hand has worked are not conducive to tightly-controlled spraying. Veteran journalist Frank Harvey visited Ranch Hand headquarters at Tan Son Nhut Airbase, Saigon, in 1967. He reported that they were flying two missions a day, six days a week. Each C-123 carried about 11,000 pounds of herbicide, worth $5,000. The herbicide was applied from a height of 150 feet at a speed of 130 knots, which is only about 15 knots faster than the speed at which a C-123 stalls and crashes. Each plane-load of herbicides was supposed to cover 300 acres.

Harvey observed that the Ranch Hand aircrews were called "magnetasses" because of their propensity for attracting ground fire, and were collecting Purple Hearts hand over fist. Their commander, Major Ralph Dresser, described coming in for Mekong-delta runs only five feet off the rice paddies and then popping up to 150 feet to spray. In the frequent event that the C-123's were threatened by ground fire or developed trouble after takeoff, their herbicide tanks could be voided in 30 seconds instead of the normal four minutes. Consequently, the many hazards of spraying missions caused herbicide douches far in excess of the standard dose, which itself was about ten times the level of usage permitted in the United States.

Defoliating base perimeters in order to deprive attackers of cover has some military logic to it. Roadside defoliation cuts two ways: the ambushers have less cover, but they can choose a site where defoliation prevents ambushed personnel from escaping the field of fire. But the slapdash broadcast-spraying of forests, fields, and villages is tactically insane. Under the best conditions, herbicides cause leaf-drop after a matter of days, but maximum defoliation occurs some months after application. Herbicides have no use in the heat of battle. Furthermore, the enemy has plenty of time to avoid regions where past herbicide use could endanger him.

As used in Indochina, herbicides have helped communist propagandists convince people that the Americans are determined to poison all elements of the Indochinese environment. In the Vietnamese districts where I worked, "American poison" was frequently mentioned with fear and loathing by farmers, though relatively little defoliation was done there. Massive defoliation is militarily useful only if the United

ECOLOGY OF DEVASTATION: INDOCHINA

States wants to drive people into population concentrations, to sever them from their natural means of livelihood, and to create inexhaustible supplies of enemies.

In June 1970 the Defense Department announced that defoliation in Indochina had been temporarily suspended two months previously. Ranch Hand's C-123s were diverted to hauling captured goods out of Cambodia, but Pentagon sources said they assumed defoliation would resume after the Cambodian incursion.

The suspension of the use of Agent Orange is still in effect at this writing. However, the use of Agent Blue to kill food crops, mainly Montagnard crops in the central highlands, has openly continued. So has the use of Agent White for defoliation.

In October 1970 Ronald Ridenhour, the same man who had exposed the My Lai massacre, discovered that the Americal Division was spraying Agent Orange on Montagnard food crops in the highlands of Quang Ngai and Quang Tin provinces. Ridenhour found this out from enlisted men in the division's 90th Chemical Detachment after their commander had claimed they were using only Agent Blue. The US command in South Vietnam subsequently admitted that Orange had been used in violation of the suspension.

In December 1970 President Nixon's press secretary, Ronald Ziegler, said that an "orderly, yet rapid phase-out" of all herbicide operations in Vietnam had begun. There are indications, however, that the Defense Department is refining its herbicide program as a means of dealing with its problems throughout the world. In 1969 the US Air Force announced that it was seeking a contractor to undertake a study toward the "ultimate goal" of a "handbook for Air Force base civil engineers with worldwide recommendations for effecting vegetation control." In the future, then, other nations may expect to be visited by "base civil engineers" ready to carry out "vegetation control" similar to that described below.

Hushed Mangroves

The Mekong River lolls sluggishly through many channels to the sea, heavy with the alluvium of numerous countries. Riding its muddy waters are mangrove seeds. In the delta, the river sediments escape the gentle thrust of the current to settle on the bottom and the mangrove seeds subsequently sprout in the new underwater soil. Soon, outposts of green arise where the land is extending into the sea.

Mangroves are not a single species. Rather, they are an aggregate of unrelated individual species, which, like members of a social class, play similar roles in a similar habitat. The pioneering mangrove species of South Vietnam is *Avicennia marina*, which colonizes the clay accretions at the sea face. The roots of *A. marina* trap and consolidate drifting soil. After five or six years, *Rhizophora conjugata*, *Bruguiera parviflora*, and *Ceriops candolleana* establish themselves on the partially stabilized soil. This process of so-called ecological succession leads, after about twenty years, to a mangrove forest dominated by *R. conjugata* and *B. parviflora*. If silting continues, the soil, enriched by dead mangroves, rises above high-tide level. Then the forest reaches its ecological climax, the final, stable stage of succession, which is dominated by the cajeput tree (*Melaleuca leucadendron*) and the nipa palm (*Nipa fruticans*).

Behind the frontier of mangrove trees, freshwater swamps develop. In these swamps a transitional ecosystem known as the hydrosere pushes the land ever farther into the water. Herbaceous aquatic plants slow the current, trap silt, and drop their dead remains. The land level rises. As conditions change, plant communities move in to be succeeded by other plants until the hydrosere reaches its climax stage, a tall forest. However, the soil beneath the forest remains exactly at water level, because the conditions for soil deposition are no longer operating.

It was this interaction between water-flow, sediment, and vegetation that created the Mekong delta. Mangrove forests presently cover about 1,800 square miles in South Vietnam, forming a bulwark against the open ocean from the tip of the Ca Mau peninsula to Cap St Jacques (Vung Tau). In addition to extending the delta land and forming the basis for the mangrove-swamp ecosystem, the mangrove trees and bushes provide useful timber, wood for making charcoal, and tannin for curing hides.

Mangrove forests have also been used as strongholds by the NLF—on the Ca Mau peninsula, at the mouth of the Saigon River, and elsewhere. Defoliants have been liberally applied to the mangroves. The AAAS Herbicide Assessment Commission estimated that by the end of 1970 about *50 percent* of the coastal mangrove forests of South Vietnam had been sprayed with herbicides. This estimate does not include the inland climax mangrove forests, sometimes referred to as rear mangroves.

Defoliated mangrove forests were also visited by USDA biologist Fred H. Tschirley and later by Gordon H. Orians and E. W. Pfeiffer. Tschirley found that *one application of herbicide kills 90 percent of trees in the mangrove type*. Orians and Pfeiffer confirmed Tschirley's observation, adding, "Most of the areas we visited by boat on the Rung Sat Peninsula were still completely barren even though some of the areas had been sprayed several years earlier. Only in occasional places was there any regeneration of mangrove trees."

Orians and Pfeiffer noted that Tschirley's estimate that it would take twenty years to reestablish the dominant mangrove forest "is based upon the assumption of immediate redistribution of seeds to the defoliated areas and the presence of suitable germination conditions when they arrive." The widespread killing of mature mangroves, they observed, inhibits seed dispersal. Also, they speculated that the "unusual soil conditions of mangrove forests may result in a failure of the herbicides to be decomposed," which could prevent seed germination. Because mangrove seeds are water-dispersed, mangrove areas flooded only by the highest tides may never be reseeded. Orians and Pfeiffer concluded, "It cannot be excluded that reestablishment of the original forest may be impossible except along the edges of the river channels."

The killing of 50 percent of South Vietnam's coastal mangroves and the consequent silencing of the profusion of life in the mangrove ecosystem may have far-reaching consequences. Mangroves are the living mechanism for the advance and protection of the land of the Mekong delta. Dr. Pfeiffer told me that he had received reports that dredging operations in the Saigon River ship channel had to be greatly increased after the mangroves died. "They defoliated there," he said, "to prevent the NLF from sinking a ship in the channel and blocking it. It worked; the mangroves were killed. But now they have to deal with the erosion. It's ironic, like the land striking back."

Spreading the Green Desert

At one time nearly all of Indochina was covered with forests. But most of these forests have been impoverished or destroyed by human activities. In the lowlands, the river deltas have been cleared of mangroves and hydroseres, and have subsequently been covered with rice paddies. Selective logging has nearly eliminated many tree species. In the highlands, *primary* (or climax) forests have been slashed and burned for swidden agriculture. Abandoned swidden fields commonly develop *secondary* forests, which are composed of fast-growing softwood species that, if left undisturbed, give way to primary-forest hardwoods after some centuries. However, soils that have been exhausted by heavy farming or overgrazing, then repeatedly swept by fire, have become either completely barren or covered with savanna grass. In such areas the former forest will never regenerate itself.

Before the Second Indochina War, forests covered about 50 percent of the two Vietnams, 25 percent of Cambodia, and 65 percent of Thailand and Laos. Extensive stands of primary forest still existed in remote areas. Since then, new and devastating factors have been applied deliberately and non-agriculturally to the forests of South Vietnam and of the border regions in Laos and Cambodia: these factors have included herbicides, explosives, Rome plows, and widespread fires.

In attempting to determine the ecological effects of these military trigger factors on the forests of South Vietnam, one must first slash through confusing forest classifications in the scientific literature. Llewelyn Williams has outlined four systems of forest classification:

1) The floristic system, in which the forest is defined by reference to the species of plants in it. For example, one often reads of South Vietnam's dipterocarp forests, which are dominated by trees of the family Dipterocarpacae.

2) The physiognomic system, in which the forest is defined by the appearance and structure of the plant community. For example, certain parts of South Vietnam have what is called triple-canopy jungle.

3) The holistic system, in which the forest is defined by all of the factors influencing it. This classification system depends on a thorough ecological study.

4) The bioclimatic system, in which the forest is defined in terms of either the seral (successional) plant community or the climax-stage plant community that is associated with a certain climate. Under this system, forest types tend to be determined by rainfall, temperature, wind, light intensity, and soil conditions.

The bioclimatic system is the commonest and certainly the clearest system for classifying tropical forests. Williams has identified eight major bioclimatic forest associations, or formations, in Southeast Asia: (a) evergreen rain forests and evergreen moist forests; (b) montane forests; (c) coniferous forests; (d) seasonal, or monsoon, forests; (e) dry deciduous forests; (f) swamp formations, composed of the brackish mangrove swamps and the freshwater hydroseres; (g) littoral formations; and (h) bamboo brakes. (The basic forest types of South Vietnam are outlined, under slightly different categories, in Table 3.)

Swamp formations already have been discussed. Littoral formations are open forests on poor seashore soils; they cover relatively small areas in South Vietnam. Bamboo brakes are seral, rather than climax, growths, and act as inhibitors of

Table 3: Forest Areas of South Vietnam.

FOREST TYPE	AREA (in 1,000 hectares)
Dense	5,530
Pure Dense (4,500)	
Dense plus Secondary (570)	
Secondary (460)	
Open	2,040
Bamboo	810
Mangrove	490
True Mangrove (330)	
Rear Mangrove (160)	
Rubber	170
Other	940
Pine (40)	
Brush (900)	
Total	9,980

Source: Presented by Arthur H. Westing to the American Association for the Advancement of Science convention, December 29, 1970 [derived from "Republic of Vietnam Vegetation Map" (Dalat: National Geographic Service, 1969)].

forest regeneration (as discussed later). Coniferous forests are limited to the Darlac plateau and apparently have not been extensively treated with herbicides. Montane forests are limited to the misty higher slopes. They grow very slowly and take at least 50 years to regenerate themselves. I have seen no studies of herbicidal effects on montane forests.

The majority of South Vietnam's forests are evergreen, seasonal, or dry deciduous formations. The evergreen forests receive at least 80 inches of rain per year, with no pronounced dry season. The seasonal forests, which are sometimes referred to as monsoon, semideciduous, or dipterocarp forests, receive between 50 and 80 inches of rain per year and have definite wet and dry seasons. In addition, they contain many deciduous trees (seasonal leaf-droppers). As annual rainfall drops below 50 inches and the dry season lengthens to six months, the seasonal forests give way to relatively open, dry deciduous forests.

Although all of South Vietnam's forest formations have received defoliants, it is the evergreen and seasonal forests that have been most extensively and repeatedly hit. These are the triple-canopy jungles of news reports, so called because they have three leafy stories. They are the forests of the Iron Triangle near Saigon and the A Shau Valley, as well as of the Ho Chi Minh Trail in Laos, the Sihanouk Trail in Cambodia, and other NLF strongholds. Defoliation research at Fort Detrick and at its test plots in Puerto Rico has concentrated on stripping these types of forests. And it is in the evergreen and seasonal forests that the consequences of herbicide use are likely to be most catastrophic.

Evergreen forests are often called tropical rain forests. "True" tropical rain forest, which receives over 100 inches of evenly-distributed rain per year, occurs in Indochina only in the Cardamom Mountains of western Cambodia. However, evergreen moist forest, with its slightly lower rainfall and longer dry season, is widely distributed in South Vietnam. Climax evergreen forests are millions of years old and their compositions have remained unchanged for thousands of years. High, even temperatures and year-round rainfall make greenhouses of these forests. Evergreen forests contain most of the genetic diversity of the Earth's plant kingdom.

Evergreen-forest plant physiognomy is shaped by upward striving for a place in the sun. The uppermost story of the triple-canopy forest is 100 to 180 feet high and is composed of the umbrella-like crowns of slender, straight trees. Below this level are two, well-defined stories with crowns and leaves shaped to absorb what light filters through the upper canopy. Within these two stories there is a profusion of lianes, which are vines that climb toward the light, and epiphytes, which are plants that live in crannies high in the trees and lianes. The dense fringe of the evergreen forest supports the popular concept of an impenetrable tropical jungle, but inside the forest the floor is quite bare and open, with few bushes and herbs living in the perpetual dusky gloom.

As evergreen forest give way to seasonal forest, the number of deciduous trees increases. There is also less variety of species and fewer lianes and epiphytes. Compared with the evergreen forest, the seasonal forest has lower stories that receive more light. Consequently, growth on the forest floor is greater. Also, the seasonal forest is more dormant during the dry season. Soil humus, which is almost entirely absent in the evergreen forest, becomes thicker as the period of dry-season dormancy increases. So the triple-story structure becomes ill-defined.

The herbicide-effect data presented below is mostly about seasonal forests, largely because biologists have not as yet given much attention to the extent of evergreen forests in South Vietnam. However, herbicides probably cause greater damage in evergreen than in seasonal forests. The microclimate of evergreen forest understories, which is maintained by constant leaf cover, is radically altered by defoliation. The possibility that certain plant species will become extinct is greater. The soil is poor, so forest regeneration is slower and may be thwarted by succession to a savanna ecosystem.

The effects of herbicides on tropical forests have been studied in test plots in Texas, Puerto Rico, and Thailand, and field investigations have been made in Tay Ninh and Binh Long provinces, northwest of Saigon. (See Table 4 for data on dessication and defoliation of rain forest vegetation caused by certain herbicides.)

One application of agents Orange or White (Purple was discontinued, because it is expensive) at the standard rate of three gallons per acre kills some of the top-story trees of a seasonal forest. Most of the herbicide is caught by the top story. A study in a two-storied Texas forest showed that 72 percent of herbicide-spray droplets were intercepted by the top story, 22 percent by the second story, and only 6 percent reached the ground. Damage to the understory is relatively slight, therefore, and such a forest can regenerate itself in several years.

Table 4: Percentage of Desiccation and Defoliation Resulting from Herbicides Applied as Low-Volume Aerial Sprays on Rain-Forest Vegetation.

Herbicide[a]	Treatment Gal/Acre	Treatment Lb/Acre	1 Wk. (%)[b]	2 Wk. (%)	1 Mo. (%)	3 Mo. (%)	6 Mo. (%)	1 Yr. (%)
Orange	1.5	12	9/3	53/28	69/61	65	52	38
	3.0	25	19/8	73/32	89/73	79	66	54
	6.0	48	28/10	79/37	89/75	91	71	61
Picloram	1.5	3	8/0	24/14	34/32	29	27	30
	3.0	6	8/0	51/21	70/52	83	60	54
	6.0	12	19/9	51/22	78/66	80	76	74
2,4,5-T Plus	1.5	7.5	7/3	25/14	42/39	52	40	45
Picloram (4:1)	3.0	15	3/0	25/5	39/32	42	46	51
(Agent White)	6.0	30	7/0	38/13	62/45	77	73	69

[a] Arrows denote typical rates.
[b] The figure to the left of the slash mark represents the percentage of leaves desiccated and defoliated; that to the right represents the percentage of defoliation. Single figures represent defoliation only.
Source: Fred H. Tschirley, 1967, in the MRI Report.

Particularly significant observations were made in a seasonal forest area of Tay Ninh province. The AAAS Herbicide Assessment Commission's report noted, "After conducting brief ground inspections at three treated sites in early 1968, Dr. Barry Flamm, Chief of the Forestry Branch (of USAID Vietnam), tentatively concluded that while a single spraying causes 10 to 20 percent killing of merchantable trees, two treatments in successive years kill 50 to 100 percent in the type of forest studied. . . . Flamm suggested further studies and recommended that forest reserves receiving two or more treatments be planned for reforestation."

A second application of herbicide during the regeneration period has a devastating impact on a seasonal forest. Orians and Pfeiffer wrote that "on sites that received two sprayings roughly 1 year apart, a heavy kill of all woody plants, including seedlings, is reported."

In 1967, Orians visited Puerto Rican test plots that had been defoliated in 1963. In plots that had received 27 pounds of herbicide per acre (Agent Orange is normally applied at 24 pounds per acre), most of the trees were killed or severely damaged. Vines had invaded the plots, climbing the dead trees and spreading out over the former canopy. "The vine-choked plots will not return to their former state as rapidly as they might otherwise," Orians and Pfeiffer wrote, "because the dead trunks will probably collapse under the weight of the vines in a few years, creating a low, vine-covered mat through which regeneration could be very difficult."

Llewelyn Williams has concisely summarized the effects that killing the primary forest have on evergreen and seasonal forest plant communities:

> In the tropical Rain forest climate, soil, vegetation, and fauna are factors that contribute to the maintenance of equilibrium in a very complex plant community. But when one of these components, such as the primary forest, is disturbed by felling and/or burning, the other components, in turn, undergo a radical change. Removal of the canopy increases the illumination at ground level from a small fraction to daylight. The range in temperature increases while

the minimum atmospheric humidity is lowered. Exposure to sun and air alter the properties of the soil. Where there are steep slopes, erosion will commence to remove the surface soil layers, and increase in soil temperature leads to a rapid disappearance of humus. The subsequent vegetation that develops becomes adjusted to the microclimate, the altered soil conditions, and to the changed conditions of the habitat.

The first phase of successional growth following the disturbance of dense, humid forest, whether in tropical America or Southeast Asia, is usually dominated by weeds and grasses. These are generally short-lived, often less than one year. The next phase may be dominated by shrubs, followed by small, soft-wooded trees. Or the succession may lead almost directly from the herbaceous stage to tree dominance. This secondary forest is usually composed in great part of trees, which are soft-wooded, of fast growth, and are wind- or animal-dispersed.

Tropical forest regeneration is slow. P. W. Richards has written, "Little is known of the time scale of secondary successions in the tropics. Chevalier (1948) states that the forest on the site of the ancient town of Angkor Wat in Cambodia, destroyed probably some five or six centuries ago, now resembles the virgin tropical forest of the district, but still shows certain differences."

Forest regeneration will be exceedingly slow in South Vietnam for a number of reasons. One reason has been emphasized by Tschirley: "The greatest danger resulting from repeated defoliation treatments in Viet Nam is that such areas will be invaded by bamboo." Bamboo is a grass. Like other grasses it is tolerant to agents Orange and White. It grows in small clumps on the floor of the forest. When the leaves of upper stories are removed, bamboo and other floor species rapidly grow in the new flood of light. Soon a thick green mat spreads over the ground, reducing horizontal visibility to almost zero and giving insurgents far more cover than they enjoyed before defoliation!

Bamboo, which primarily reproduces vegetatively from underground stems, is almost impossible to eradicate from soil it has invaded. Bamboo brakes cover many abandoned swidden plots in South Vietnam and are also taking over heavily defoliated areas. Tschirley, who made ground observations near Special Forces camps, has written that "seedlings were rare in dense bamboo, but frequent to numerous where there was no bamboo. Probably of more importance is the fact that saplings were rare in dense bamboo."

Forest regeneration will be particularly slow in areas treated by Agent White. White is a mixture of 2,4-D and picloram. In their article about picloram, George R. Harvey and Jay D. Mann noted that picloram is the most active herbicide yet discovered. Picloram is generally more than 100 times as biologically active as 2,4-D. When used even in very small doses it will kill a wide range of broad-leaved crops. In 1968, Agent White accounted for about 35 percent of herbicide use in South Vietnam.

Harvey and Mann quoted Dr. C. E. Minarik of Fort Detrick as saying that White was used in South Vietnam because it "controls conifers." However, the rather small coniferous forest on the Darlac plateau has apparently escaped defoliation. More relevant is Harvey and Mann's quotation of a Defense Department study done by Tschirley: "A few species tolerate high rates of picloram but many species tolerate high rates of other herbicides. Thus the use of picloram is particularly appropriate for the defoliation of forest types characterized by high species diversity. Such forest types are frequently found in tropical environments."

In addition to being able to kill a wide range of plant species, picloram is one of the most persistent herbicides. While 2,4-D and 2,4,5-T are broken down by soil microorganisms after a few weeks, picloram remains active in the soil for several months before *any* disappearance can be detected. Puerto Rican test plots treated with picloram remained essentially bare of leaves for *two years*, at which time inspections were discontinued.

Another factor that will retard forest regeneration in South Vietnam was mentioned by Dr. Arthur H. Westing at the AAAS convention in December 1970. Most of the trees in seasonal and evergreen forests in the tropics are dicotyledonous. Dicotyledonous trees have an opportunity to reseed only once in several decades, at the time of general flowering and stem death. This period of delayed forest regeneration is sometimes called a secondary climax. Its length is not precisely known. Westing suggested further inquiry into the matter.

As mentioned earlier, the Defense Department has not yet released its records of which areas of South Vietnam have been sprayed with which herbicides. On the basis of other evidence, however, Westing has tentatively concluded that 35 percent of South Vietnam's 14 million acres of dense (evergreen and seasonal) forests had been sprayed by December 1970. Westing also estimated that 25 percent had been sprayed once and 10 percent more than once. Based on these educated guesses, Westing estimated the cash value of the destroyed timber to be $470 million; that would be enough timber to meet South Vietnam's needs for 31 years.

The forests of South Vietnam have not been merely damaged for decades or centuries to come. Nor have they simply been deprived of rare tree species. It is probable that many areas will experience an ecosystem succession under which forest will be replaced by savanna.

Swidden farmers have already created savannas in various parts of Indochina by slashing and burning the forest and then exhausting the soil through frequent planting. If such impoverished land is regularly burned it becomes grassland dotted with a few stunted, fire-resistant bushes. This is called a fire-climax savanna, because if fires are prevented the forest will slowly regenerate itself. Natural and man-made fires frequently sweep these savannas, stopping at the edge of the humid evergreen and seasonal forests. If the savanna is overgrazed, as has been the case in large areas of northern Africa, the soil is completely exhausted and becomes desert. The process is aptly termed Saharization.

Dr. Pfeiffer told me that succession to savanna probably would not occur in South Vietnam, owing to the rapid regrowth of bamboo and brush. He suggested that if savannas were created, it would be likely to happen in areas repeatedly defoliated by Agent White. However, the bombs, artillery fire, and napalm flung about in defoliated forests cause them to burn over and over. Furthermore, repeated defoliation that kills broad swaths of forests also prevents trees from reseeding because all seed sources are dead. It is likely, therefore, that American military tactics in South Vietnam are probably creating many green deserts.

Tropical forests should be treated as international treasures rather than as objects of devastating, futile wrath. As P. W. Richards has written, they are "a reservoir of genetical diversity and potential variability." Tropical evergreen forests, like so many other features of the world environment, may become extinct before humanity fully understands their value.

Crop Destruction

It is difficult to select the most morally repugnant tactic of the Second Indochina War, but the use of American aircraft to destroy food crops is a strong contender for that foul distinction. In 1962, when the South Vietnamese Government announced plans to spray manioc and sweet-potato fields, the American military officially disassociated itself from that program. By 1968, though, the US Air Force announced that it had covered about half a million acres of food crops with the dessicant Agent Blue. At that time, crop destruction made up about 15 percent of the total herbicidal effort. The spraying of Agent Blue on food crops continues at this writing.

In December 1970, the AAAS Herbicide Assessment Commission observed, "Somewhat more than 2,000 square kilometers of cropland is reported to have been sprayed. If little of this area includes respraying, it would represent about five percent of the 38,000 square kilometers of crop land in South Vietnam of which a little over two percent was sprayed in the peak year of 1967."

Field spraying is part of what is commonly called the food-denial program, the object of which is to starve insurgents into submission. A related tactic employed by American forces is the destruction of rice stores found in rural areas.

ECOLOGY OF DEVASTATION: INDOCHINA

To the extent that food denial is effective, it starves the weaker noncombatants. As Dr. Jean Mayer, who has observed numerous famines, wrote:

> Whatever method is used, the examination of past wars and famines makes it clear that the food shortage will strike first and hardest at children, the elderly, and pregnant and lactating women; last and least at adult males, and least of all at soldiers. . . . The history of modern war has been one of increasing involvement of civilians. Starvation as a weapon is an aspect of such involvement, one which has the peculiar property of inflicting suffering on civilians while doing little damage to the military.

Crop destruction also contributes to the forced-draft urbanization social policy. According to Presidential science adviser Donald F. Hornig, rice destruction is designed to force farmers into the US-GVN sphere of influence. This policy is particularly brutal because all admitted crop spraying is done in rural areas of the central highlands, where almost all crops are grown by Montagnard villagers.

Malnutrition and related diseases, widespread under the best conditions in Indochina, are particularly common among Montagnard tribespeople. Isolated from the national economy, growing low-yield swidden crops, and lacking medical care, the Montagnards exist with death close at their sides. NLF taxation efforts, combined with American air strikes and crop destruction, often force Montagnards into lowland refugee camps. There they are landless, wracked by disease in a strange climate, and under the power of hostile Vietnamese. (See the full discussion of this topic in Chapter 5.) Americans pushing so-called model refugee villages for Montagnards have often awakened to find that their guests have left *en masse* to face death on their home ground. To many highland tribes the Second Indochina War is genocidal. The US crop-destruction program is a vicious means of bringing whole human cultures close to extinction.

Dr. Meselson of the AAAS team estimated that 600,000 people, most of them Montagnards, had been cut off from their normal food supplies by crop spraying. Meselson told the AAAS convention in December 1970 that he had flown over a cultivated valley in the central highlands where the land had recently been sprayed with herbicides. Analysis of aerial photographs of the valley revealed 940 houses along the spray zone. In discussion at the convention, General William Stone, who recently directed the US Army's Chemical and Nuclear Operations, said the houses had long been abandoned. Meselson said he had seen what he thought were signs of current occupation.

If the houses Meselson saw were abandoned, it was probably because crop destruction had forced their Montagnard occupants to move. The US Army clearly knew, in 1967, that crop-killing herbicides were destroying civilian food supplies and having almost no effect on NLF food supplies. At least those in the US Army who had access to social science studies of the effects of crop spraying on the NLF knew that all findings indicated that only civilians were being harmed by field spraying. By the fall of 1970 there were five such studies in US Army hands. That the military continues to spray crops at this writing indicates the extent to which environmental devastation has escaped rational political control.

Two of the studies were done by the Rand Corporation for the Advanced Research Projects Agency (ARPA), which is the Defense Department's research arm. The first study was based on interviews with prisoners and defectors. It found that some NLF-NVA troops had ample rations, some had barely enough, and that only about five percent of them depended on local crops for food. It also found that there was no relationship between crop spraying and ration size in any area. The second study showed that almost all prisoners who said they had surrendered because of hunger claimed their hunger did not result from crop spraying. It also showed that wind-drift from herbicide spraying was seriously affecting civilian farmers. Both of these studies were completed in October 1970 and were classified as confidential.

The third study, done in December 1967 by the scientific adviser to the US military Pacific command (CINCPAC), included quotations from prisoners and several pages of statements by American officers who praised the herbicide program. The study's facts showed that herbicide had damaged the crops of one South Vietnamese out of every 400, but through an "error in arithmetic" it concluded that "fewer than one South Vietnamese in 40,000" had his crops destroyed.

The fourth study, done by the US military command and US Embassy in South Vietnam, drew upon the so-called arithmetic error of the third study. It also showed that as much as 99 percent of all food had been destroyed in some provinces. Both the third and fourth studies concluded that herbicide operations should be continued.

The fifth study, undertaken by the US military command in South Vietnam, indicated that only about one percent of enemy troops got food from their own farming efforts, while many more lived off civilian crops.

Though purposeful crop destruction is supposedly confined to the central highlands, widespread field spraying has occurred throughout the central coastal valleys and the Mekong delta. This is "accidental" crop destruction by the defoliants Orange and White, which are toxic to a large number of broad-leaved crops and fruit trees. These auxin, or hormone, herbicides also kill rice and other cereal crops when the plants are just emerging from the ground or when they are beginning to flower. As Harvey and Mann noted, Agent White is particularly dangerous to rice, because "a persistent auxin herbicide like picloram can be expected to injure rice when it germinates, or if used after germination, to severely hinder seed development."

Orians and Pfeiffer reported that the defoliation program was reviewed in 1967, owing to the overwhelming number of crop-damage claims. The US then began using Agent White for most of its Mekong delta defoliation, because White does not drift with the wind as readily as does Orange. "Nevertheless," wrote Orians and Pfeiffer, "we encountered many reports of very recent damage in that area."

The reasons for that damage are not difficult to ascertain.

Although White is less likely to waft for miles during spraying, it does contain picloram. According to Harvey and Mann, "The persistence and stability of picloram are such that after application to an area 'where accurate spraying is essential,' it can be washed or the vapors blown to untreated land. Vietnam is not lacking in either heavy rain or wind."

The major targets of defoliation in the Mekong delta, beginning with the first defoliation tests in 1961, have been the banks and sides of rivers, canals, and roads. The Mekong delta looks like a broad green quilt of rice fields, segmented by the slightly raised land alongside waterways and roads. People build their homes strung out along these transportation routes and use roadsides and channel banks to grow fruit trees and broad-leaved garden crops. In other words, *defoliation targets in the Mekong delta include human habitations, fruit trees, and garden crops.*

Plants near the American bases splayed about Saigon, which themselves look like movie sets on Asteroid 69, have suffered particularly intensive poisoning. In that area it is difficult to distinguish among the effects of spraying around the bases, jettisoned defoliant loads, jet-exhaust fumes, and the excretions of scooters burning heavily oiled fuel. Orians and Pfeiffer observed damage to many fruit trees in Ho Nai, a Catholic village near Bien Hoa airbase. They noted that defoliants had been dumped by an aircraft in trouble in the area at about the same time that spray came down on the village. Residents of Ho Nai claimed they had been bathed with defoliants seven times in the past year. Orians and Pfeiffer added, "The experimental station of the College of Agriculture of the University of Saigon at Tu Duc has been affected by wind-blown defoliants several times, usually with almost complete kill of vegetables."

In Saigon itself, most trees lining the streets have died, presumably killed by motor-vehicle exhaust fumes. The National Park, founded in 1864, has nursed over 2,000 species of foreign and domestic plants. Nguyen Thuoc of Dispatch News International quoted plant expert Truong Dau as saying, "The 100-year-old tree in the Park, the Thorpay Dapap, died some months ago. Over two-thirds of the old trees, over 80 years old, in the Park are dead. There are almost no old trees left. If we wish to have trees like those, we must wait another century." The death of plants in this botanical garden is a particularly bitter blow, for such gardens are the means of establishing and studying valuable plant species throughout the tropical world.

A plant that originated in Brazil and was spread from European botanical gardens to become a major export crop of South Vietnam, Cambodia, and other tropical nations, is the rubber tree. In 1968, the US Army Chemical Operations Division was maintaining that rubber trees cannot be killed by defoliants. Yet, after field examination and review of studies, Pfeiffer has concluded that rubber, jackfruit, and other latex-producing trees are *especially susceptible* to auxin herbicides. Orians and Pfeiffer wrote:

> Accidental defoliations in Vietnam indicate that trees less than 7 years old can be killed by the dosages used in military operations, but that older trees normally recover. Nevertheless, all trees on 100 hectares on Plantation Ben Cui were killed by herbicides in 1965, despite the fact that the trees were 33 years old. From such occurrences, the Rubber Research Institute concluded that repeated defoliations threaten the very existence of rubber culture in Vietnam.

During 1967-68, the staff of the Rubber Research Institute of Viet Nam visited over 200 rubber plantations in the great arc of red soils between the Mekong delta and the central highlands. They found that all plantations reported damage by defoliants and that more than 40,000 hectares (98,800 acres) of rubber were defoliated at least 10 percent. Owing to defoliation and other depredations of war, South Vietnam's rubber yield dropped from 77,560 dry tons in 1960 to 42,510 dry tons in 1967. Because defoliated rubber trees are further weakened or killed if tapped for latex, only large planters who can afford to take damaged trees out of production are still in the rubber business in South Vietnam.

Damage to South Vietnam's rubber trees has been traced to wind-drift of forest defoliants. In 1969, during April and early May, great swaths of rubber trees were defoliated by direct overflight in Cambodia, which was then a precariously neutral country. This defoliation was confirmed by a US State Department team and later by an international investigating group. The international group found that 70,000 hectares (173,000 acres) of rubber trees had been damaged and that about 10,000 hectares (24,700 acres) of this area had been severely damaged. The damaged rubber trees in production amounted to over one-third of all Cambodia's producing rubber trees at that time. As a result of this defoliation, the economic loss to Cambodia between May and November 1969 was estimated to be $11 million. The group reported that the pattern of damage to the rubber trees "forced us to the conclusion that at least two-thirds of the actual damage in Cambodia was the result of direct overflight." Devastation of a wide variety of fruit trees and garden crops was also observed in the area.

Dr. Pfeiffer, a member of the international investigating group, has made many efforts to discover which US agency defoliated these Cambodian rubber plantations. "The US is still negotiating to pay $12 million in damages to Cambodia," he told me, "but nobody seems to know who did it. Ranch Hand says it wasn't their planes." Pfeiffer considers it strange that the US can wreak such destruction without officially knowing which of its governmental arms struck the blow, and he encourages people to join him in making inquiries. By now, of course, Cambodia's rubber production has almost ceased and its rubber-processing factories have been bombed into rubble.

Depth interviews of sixty farmers and village officials throughout South Vietnam were done for the AAAS Herbicide Assessment Commission by Samuel Popkin of Harvard University's Center for International Affairs. Dr. Popkin reported at the December 1970 convention that "farmers feel that herbicides have made a serious impact on their crops." Most damage seemed to result from spray drift. The farmers,

Popkin found, could distinguish herbicide damage from other harm to their crops, but were vague about the effects of herbicides on farm animals. He noted that the number of crop-damage compensation claims, which are paid off by the South Vietnamese Government with US funds, "is a very inadequate guide to the extent of actual damage caused by herbicides." After describing the red tape of the compensation process (the forms are filled out incorrectly, the bribes must be paid, etc.), Popkin added, "Since there is widespread propaganda by the U.S. and South Vietnamese stating that herbicides affect only those in communist areas, many peasants are afraid that an application for compensation will be interpreted politically as an anti-government gesture."

During 1967 and 1968, I had a chance to participate in this compensation process. In the province where I worked, a Vietnamese committee was given a fixed sum to distribute as compensation for herbicide damage. This sum was allocated among the various districts on a rotating basis, with two or three districts receiving the full payment for one year. Claims had no relation to crop damage, crop planting, or even land ownership, although some attempt was made to keep allegedly damaged areas from overlapping on the map. The administrating committee made no effort to investigate claims on the ground. Indeed, its members felt unsafe from the moment they deplaned in our insecure little valley.

Of the three Montagnard resettlement villages I was working with, two received paltry damage-compensation checks and the third received nothing, even though the claims of the third were equally valid—that is, totally fabricated. I flew with those checks to two distant cities above very insecure roads, first to have them endorsed and then to have them cashed. One village tried to have their checks cashed on their own, but were refused payment until I applied my American *persona* to bank officials. I couldn't help recalling that unless the Vietnamese province chief had requested a defoliation mission, that good loose money never would have flowed into the province.

THE GREEN DEVOLUTION

Land Deform in the Mekong Delta

[Control of the Mekong delta is one of the chief prizes at stake in the Second Indochina War.] Counterinsurgents often speak of preventing the communist bloc from controlling "Asia's rice bowl." Though rice production in the Mekong delta is not large enough to be rationally considered vital to feeding China, much less America, it could balance the industrial production of North Vietnam to make a reunited Vietnam economically viable.

The delta is a massive rice-culture plate, where plant ecology has been distorted by humanity to produce more human nutrition. The carrying capacity of the delta, its ability to produce plants valuable to mankind, is a matter of great importance to the Vietnamese people. Because the delta environment is maintained by constant human intervention, study of its ecology involves a look at human society in relation to delta cropland.

Clifford Geertz has noted, "The micro-ecology of the flooded paddy field has yet to be written." Much is known about efficiently producing rice for maximum benefit to humanity. This is because people see a rice field as a generator of value rather than as an ecosystem.

The flooded rice field as an economically valuable ecosystem has certain unique characteristics. It is a very stable producer of crops, able to bring forth one or two crops per year for centuries without being exhausted. Its productivity is not decreased by overcultivation caused by population pressure or other factors. A rice paddy is almost infinitely receptive to improved cultivation techniques. More careful nursing brings forth ever-higher yields.

Maintenance of a rice field depends on two factors. The first is availability of water in precise quantity and of certain content. As Geertz has explained:

> Here, the characteristic thinness of tropical soils is circumvented through the bringing of nutrients onto the terrace by the irrigation water to replace those drawn from the soil; through the fixation of nitrogen by the blue-green

algae which proliferate in the warm water; through the chemical and bacterial decomposition of organic material, including the remains of harvested crops in that water; through the aeration of the soil by the gentle movement of the water in the terrace; and, no doubt, through other ecological functions performed by irrigation which are as yet unknown.

It is probable (as discussed in Chapter 4) that water content and rate of water supply in South Vietnam are being altered by watershed forest defoliation and craterization.

The second, closely-related factor necessary for the maintenance of a rice field is intensive cultivation by people. Left alone, a rice field quickly reverts to a natural ecosystem. Restoration of abandoned rice fields demands considerable investment. In some cases (also discussed in Chapter 4), it may be impossible.

Application of the Devastation Model of counterinsurgency, aimed at driving farmers from the land, has, according to the Joint Development Group, taken about 300,000 hectares (about 750,000 acres) of cropland out of cultivation in South Vietnam. As was obvious in the central coastal valley where I worked, the dangers and resource-diversions of war also prevent the opening of new land and the maintenance of irrigation systems.

Rice land is economic value. In this war of many faces, power to distribute the production of rice fields has been a major issue, and probably the most important issue, of the war in the Mekong delta. We now have an excellent study of the economic structure of the Mekong delta as it relates to the war: *The Economics of Insurgency* by Robert L. Sansom. The findings of Sansom's study will provide the backdrop for a discussion of the land-reform program passed by the Thieu government in March 1970.

Between 1868 and 1930 the cultivated area in the Mekong delta grew from 215,000 to 2,214,000 hectares. The delta was converted into rice land by the French, who had drainage canals dug through its swamps and forests, and by Vietnamese developers, who acquired title to land along the canals. The developers hired laborers to dig ditches to connect to the canals, thereby draining the land of brackish, stagnant water. Brush and trees were cut and then burned to enrich the soil. Dikes were raised to block the dry-season ocean tides. Finally, the developers recruited tenant farmers, charging them up to 70 percent of their crops in rent.

By 1930 there was no more new land to develop. The area under cultivation in the Mekong delta actually declined after that date, dropping drastically after 1946 and again after 1965 as the two Indochina wars swept the countryside. Meanwhile, the population of the delta increased from about 4,500,000 in 1931 to 9,000,000 by the early 1960s. The per-acre crop yield remained low. In 1961, according to Sansom's calculations, 1,000,000, or about 77 percent, of the delta's farmers were tenants and about 2,000,000 of the delta's residents were landless laborers.

Sansom outlined three phases in the recent development of landholding relationships in the Mekong delta. The first phase began in 1946 as the Viet Minh assumed control of much of the delta and concluded in 1954 with the installation of Premier, later President, Ngo Dinh Diem. During this phase the Viet Minh used terror and public trial to drive landlords to the cities, redistribute much land to tenants and landless laborers, and reduce rent on land still controlled by landlords. Between 1954 and 1959, the Diem government halted or reversed this expropriation. Landlords followed the GVN back into the countryside or, as happened frequently, simply had GVN village officials, with the aid of the military, collect their rents for a 30 percent commission.

In 1960 the NLF commenced a campaign of rent suppression and land redistribution. By 1966 the NLF was enforcing rents at 5–10 percent of the crop over 70 percent of the delta's land. In GVN-held areas, rents stayed above 25 percent, as they had since 1954, despite a GVN law designed to hold rents at 25 percent or lower. In addition, the NLF had redistributed much land in areas under their control. Sansom has observed, "From all the benefits it brought to the peasantry, it can probably be said that the impetus behind the Viet Cong land reform was not in the general case terror but the sanction of implied force supported by the general will."

It was clear by the late sixties that the landlord-tenant system, which had evolved from a means of opening new land to a system of depriving a growing population of the fruits of their labor, could not be reestablished in the delta by any power. Decree 57, a land-reform law passed by the Diem government in 1956, had affected only ten percent of the delta's tenants and was evaded by such tactics as distribution of land to the landlord's relatives. In contrast, the NLF, with the support of the delta's tenants and laborers, gained the initiative in land policy in most of the delta despite the military assaults of the Second Indochina War. Landlords had lost control over most of their titular holdings and could look forward to further property losses as the US withdrew. It is against this background that, on March 26, 1970, the Thieu government passed its "Land to the Tiller" land-reform law.

The Thieu land-reform law, widely praised in the American press, will stand as another example of the perils of underestimating the cynical opportunism of the Saigon regime. The US has already agreed to put up $10 million for the program and it is hard to see how the financially foundering GVN can meet its grandiose $1.2 billion land-reform budget without huge dollar gifts. In essence, the law provides that landlords will be paid for land to which they hold title and that the land will be redistributed to farmers, three hectares per family in the delta and one hectare per family in central South Vietnam. As Duong Son Quan pointed out in an article in the August 1970 issue of *Tu Quyet*, a Saigon magazine, "The great majority of the lands to be taken away from the landlords lie in areas with no security or where security is limited, since lands in secure areas have already either been taken away by Decree 57 or the landlords have found ways of dividing them to their descendants." In other words, the landlords will be paid for land already out of their control, land where either the NLF holds sway or the war prevents cultivation. As Quan put it, "The end result is that only the landlords benefit much from the whole thing, since they are being paid 161.22 billion piasters for paddy fields that have not yielded anything for a long time, while the government, after spending 161.22 billions, is still unable to control the peasants."

At the bottom of the priority list for land distribution, following such categories as retired GVN officials and GVN personnel who had to abandon farming because of the war, are landless laborers. These laborers represent the Mekong delta class that has the greatest need for land and that is the firmest source of NLF support. And, as Quan observed, if land recipients have the temerity to brave NLF policies and American bombs to farm their new land, they will be forced to borrow from the landlords in order to restore land to cultivation. "Thus the old situation will repeat itself exactly as before," wrote Quan. "Financial dependency will lead to physical and psychological dependency."

During his field observations in the Mekong delta, Sansom found that a technological as well as a landholding revolution had occurred during the sixties. Improved strains of rice had been introduced. The invention of a small water pump had made vegetable-growing possible and had permitted the growing of two rice crops per year on many fields. The rice strains, Sansom noted, were spread by individual Vietnamese farmers and the water pump (which AID engineers denounced as "inefficient") was invented by a Vietnamese. Sansom concluded that delta Vietnamese are not inhibited by their culture from applying the best available agricultural techniques. I agree, and add that the generally well-meaning efforts of American technicians to feed miracle rice, fertilizer, and other agricultural improvements through corrupt GVN bureaucracies to the peasants are, at best, not necessary.

Despite all American efforts to spread the Green Revolution and despite Vietnamese technological innovations, South Vietnam continues to import American rice. The war itself, causing field destruction, interruption of transportation, and population dislocation, is the major factor inhibiting agricultural development in the Mekong delta. Survival of US-GVN programs in the delta is made possible only by waging a war that deforms the land and cancels what benefits delta residents could receive from Western technology. The war also keeps alive the last vestiges of a deformed, exploitative human system of distributing the produce of the delta. Mr. Quan summed up the problem of land reform in the Mekong delta quite simply: "As long as the war is still going on, the problem of tenant farming will still exist; when the war comes to an end, tenant farming will end with it."

CHAPTER THREE

War Upon the Animals

The NLF frequently attacks villages by night for the sole purpose of killing all dogs, because the barking of dogs is the warning system of village defenders. Once the First Cavalry tried to capture some "VC water buffaloes" (buffaloes loose in a remote area) to donate them to Montagnard refugees. The First Cavalry forces broke off contact after hours of chasing and rope-waving, returning in an empty Chinook helicopter to declare the buffaloes victorious. The buffaloes of South Vietnam, quite docile when approached by Vietnamese, often lunge with rage at Americans.

Unlike dogs and buffaloes, most of the fauna of Indochina are politically neutral. Yet in this war against ecosystems, animals are among the victims. As the international group that investigated defoliation in Cambodia reported, some beasts have even become refugees:

> It is interesting to note here that eastern Cambodia in general has experienced quite a substantial increase in a variety of wildlife, apparently driven out of Vietnam by the defoliation and other ravages of war. Included are mutjacs and other species of deer, wild cattle (gaurs, bantengs, and some koupreys), elephants, a number of monkey species, and wild pigs.

Now that the war has been brought to eastern Cambodia these animals must feel as stripped of refuge as do the peoples of Indochina.

ECOLOGY OF DEVASTATION: INDOCHINA

In the energy-pyramid of life, animals constitute trophic levels 2, 3, and 4—which are the herbivore level and the two carnivores levels. (Animals are also among the decomposers of trophic level 5, which is discussed in Chapter 4.) Little attention has been devoted to the wartime fate of animals. Scattered reports and ecological studies indicate, however, that Indochina's fauna have been substantially damaged by the war. The destruction of green plants, depriving the fauna of food and shelter, has killed certain animal species over large areas. Because of the interdependence of plants and animals —a mutual reliance that is especially important in tropical forests—the defoliation-caused death of fauna can in turn inhibit forest regeneration. In addition, defoliants are directly toxic to a number of animals, many of which provide Indochinese people with sustenance. Poisoning and habitat-destruction pose a threat to the continued existence of rare species, only a few of which are probably known to science.

Orians and Pfeiffer, both zoologists, were particularly concerned with the effects that the destruction of mangroves had on wildlife. During their visit to the Rung Sat mangrove area, they saw no insect-eating or fruit-eating birds other than barn swallows, which had migrated there from the north. They saw some fish-eating birds, though fewer than they had expected. They concluded that tree destruction had affected aquatic food chains less severely than it had terrestrial food cycles.

Orians and Pfeiffer also noted that many birds and animals are restricted to a mangrove habitat. "These animals," they wrote, "are therefore inhabitants of 'islands' surrounded by unsuitable habitat and as such are expected to have higher rates of extinction even under normal conditions than species of more continuous habitats." Because great areas of mangroves have been killed by single applications of Agent Orange, many animal species on the Mekong delta coast have probably become locally extinct.

Aquatic fauna living in the channels winding through the mangroves probably have been severely damaged by tree destruction (though no investigation of this matter has yet been made). These animals, as Dr. Westing noted at the AAAS convention in December 1970, rely directly or indirectly on nutrients flowing from the mangrove vegetation.

In a tropical evergreen or seasonal forest, most plant and animal species are concentrated in the upper stories. In many ways the continued existence of tropical-forest fauna depends on the forest canopy remaining intact. Many forest species cannot adapt to secondary-forest growth. As a group of Stanford University biologists wrote, "Defoliation or killing of vast areas of forest is an event unprecedented in the evolutionary history of any tropical species. Even several months of defoliation in the forests of Vietnam is certain to cause the extinction of many animal populations."

Two Vietnamese species of primates, the Douc langur and the Indochinese gibbon, were known to be endangered with extinction even before defoliation. As these animals live in tropical forest trees (the Douc langur eats only leaves), defoliation may have wiped them out.

While many species of tropical-forest fauna depend on an undisturbed leaf canopy for their survival, many types of forest plants rely on fauna for pollination and seed dispersal. A number of tropical-forest tree species are outbreeding. That is, they can reproduce only by obtaining pollen from another tree of the same species, even though individual trees of the same species are widely separated from one another. Such trees are fertilized by "traplining" insects and birds, which regularly fly great distances to feed on the flowers of a certain species of tree. For example, Euglossine bees of tropical forests cover five- or ten-mile "traplines," feeding on plants that produce a few flowers per day over a period of months. Many tropical-forest plants are pollinated over long periods by a lacework of specific "traplining" fauna.

Seed dispersal in tropical forests is also heavily reliant on fauna. For example, *Miconia*, a genus of plants in tropical America, depends on birds for distributing its seeds. The eighteen *Miconia* species in Trinidad space their fruiting seasons in such a way that the birds have a constant food supply and the plants do not compete with each other for seed-dispersal agents.

Ecologists are only beginning to study complex plant-animal relationships in climax tropical forests, where evolution has occurred in a mild, regular climate over a period of millions of years. Defoliation destroys the microclimate of forest understories. Tree destruction over large areas will probably prevent regeneration of any trees whose seeds are dispersed by animals. (The dipterocarp trees that dominate many regenerating forests in Indochina are reseeded by the wind.) Herbicides, intended only to cause leaves to fall, can have destructive consequences for plants and animals far from the zone of application.

In addition to destroying animal habitats in Indochina, herbicides are toxic to the animals themselves. Assessment of the toxicity of herbicides is a subject fraught with contradiction, confusion, and reliance on inconclusive studies. Habitat destruction caused by herbicides will probably have a greater and longer lasting effect on Indochinese animals than will direct herbicidal poisoning. Nevertheless, testing has shown that all herbicides used in Indochina are toxic in certain amounts to certain organisms.

Numerous reports that herbicides have killed farm animals and fish circulate in South Vietnam. Vietnamese testimony presented to the Russell war-crimes tribunal alleged that aerial spray had caused rapid sickness and death in livestock that ate affected plants, and that it had also killed fish. Similar testimony is frequently distributed by the NLF. The NLF also publishes number-of-persons-poisoned figures, which ran about 300,000 per year from 1966 through 1969. (Herbicide toxicity to humans is discussed in Chapter 5.)

Orians and Pfeiffer heard reports of birds and animals being killed by herbicides, but brief bird-netting expeditions near Saigon disclosed a profusion of lustily-singing birds in a recently defoliated area. Where I worked in South Vietnam the farmers tended to blame all natural misfortunes on "American poison," because the NLF encouraged this point of view and American compensation might be forthcoming.

Not all of these claims can be discounted as balderdash or propaganda. The MRI Report contains the only summary of herbicide-toxicity studies I have seen. The conclusions in the report are more blandly reassuring than are the data presented. South Vietnam is not a laboratory, although the experimental testing value of the war has been noticed by counterinsurgents of various stripes. Herbicides are sprayed not only on fields and forests, but on villages and waterways as well. The heavy concentrations of spray and the large areas sprayed in South Vietnam are without precedent, so we may expect herbicides to have unprecedented toxic effects on animals there.

The MRI Report judged that the chemical 2,4-D, which makes up 50 percent of Agent Orange, is dangerous to freshwater food chains. The report cited a study indicating that one part per million (ppm) of 2,4-D in fresh water "gives about 43% reduction in weight of fish food in one week and about 90% in one year." A table in the report shows that at the level of spraying used in South Vietnam, 2,4-D would concentrate in amounts far in excess of one ppm in flooded rice fields and small canals.

Orians and Pfeiffer presented the results of testing 2,4-D on baby salmon. They noted that 2,4-D applied to a small stream in military volume would fill the water with over 100 times the LD_{50} (dose lethal to 50 percent of the salmon). The fish of the rice fields and canals are second only to rice as sources of food for Vietnamese peasants and they supply most of the protein in rural Vietnamese diets. Orians and Pfeiffer called for investigation of reported damage to freshwater fish. They noted, "Conditions in the shallow water of the fields are ideal for concentration of herbicides." Although 2,4-D is rapidly inactivated, it could do much damage to freshwater organisms in a short time.

Certain plants become poisonous after being treated with 2,4-D. As Orians and Pfeiffer explained:

> Sublethal dosages of 2,4-D may markedly affect the metabolism of certain plant species so that toxic quantities of

nitrates accumulate in the treated plants. In the animals the nitrates are changed to nitrites which are absorbed into the blood producing methemoglobin which results in oxygen deficiency to the tissues. This condition may cause death or illness resulting in abortion. . . . A recent statement by an American agricultural specialist emphasizes that "Dairy cows should not be grazed on irrigated pasture for seven days after application of 2,4-D at the one-half pound and over rate of application."

The MRI Report summed up its review of 2,4,5-T, an ingredient of agents Orange and Purple, by saying, "In summary, 2,4,5-T resembles 2,4-D in its toxicity to animals and fish but is a little more toxic." Also, 2,4,5-T is highly teratogenic (fetus-deforming), as determined by tests on rat and chicken embryos (a matter discussed more fully in Chapter 5).

Picloram, when combined with 2,4-D to make Agent White, yields a combination that is more toxic to mammals than is either chemical alone. The MRI Report stated that "picloram would be rated as nontoxic . . . [but Agent White] would be rated as mildly toxic on the basis of the toxicity designation presented in the USDA Agriculture Handbook 332 (1067)." The compound separates in water, thereby freeing the 2,4-D to do its work on underwater organisms.

Cacodylic acid, the active ingredient of the crop-killing Agent Blue, is an organic arsenical compound. The MRI Report cited a study that "describes cacodylic acid as a material which has medicinal properties similar to those of inorganic arsenic 'to which it is partly reduced in the body.' Since the reduction is slow the toxicity is reduced but the effects last longer." The Ansul Chemical Company, after observing the effects of this arsenical compound on its workers, pronounced its toxicity "relatively low." Nevertheless, the MRI Report writers have suggested that, "In view of the absence of long-term feeding studies or of reproduction studies, we feel that these should be undertaken soon."

The MRI Report noted that arsenical compounds have long been considered carcinogenic (cancer-causing) and cited an experiment in which injected cacodylic acid caused "profound disturbance of cell division" in mice. Cacodylic acid is also considered to be teratogenic. Arsenical insecticides are highly toxic to bees (there are a number of Vietnamese beekeepers), but apparently cacodylic acid never has been tested on bees.

Lest we grow alarmed about spraying arsenic on food, people, and water, the MRI Report reassures us: "The presence of toxic residues on rice from sprayed fields appears not to be a problem since no rice develops in these fields." One scientist injected cacodylic acid into a tree infested with bark beetles. "The trees died," said the report, "but so did 84 to 99% of the bark beetles; the author suggests this procedure as a possible method of controlling this beetle." We had to destroy the tree in order to save it!

Dr. Westing told the AAAS convention in December 1970 that he had sprayed chickens with herbicides and that the chickens had not died. Westing also noted that more acres in South Vietnam had been sprayed with the insecticide Malathion (to kill malaria-bearing mosquitoes) than had been sprayed with herbicides. He remarked that chicken deaths reported by Vietnamese farmers might have resulted from Malathion overdoses. Malathion is known to be highly toxic to honeybees.

Some animals are able to adapt to the war. Urban conditions are ideal for the proliferation of rats. Orians and Pfeiffer wrote, "The Tan Son Nhut air base in Saigon is sprayed by hand with agent Blue several times each year and nonetheless has a serious rat problem." Although many forest beasts suffer from lack of food, Orians and Pfeiffer reported that tigers are getting along quite nicely:

> In the past 24 years, they have learned to associate the sounds of gunfire with the presence of dead and wounded human beings in the vicinity. As a result, tigers rapidly move toward gunfire and apparently consume large numbers of battle casualties. Although there are no accurate statistics on the tiger populations past or present, it is likely that the tiger population has increased much as the wolf population in Poland increased during World War II.

ECOLOGY OF DEVASTATION: INDOCHINA

Marine Colonel William R. Corson, in his book about how to win the war in Vietnam, described one of his campaigns "to show the peasant that by combining or exploiting these resources he could maintain a financially rewarding existence." After winning the confidence of the people of Phong Bac hamlet by playing Chinese chess with them, Corson hired a number of Vietnamese fishermen and rented their boats. An amazed crowd watched as Corson and his men threw explosives into the Song Cau Do River, collected stunned fish with the help of their hirelings, sold the fish, and turned the money over to a newly-declared "hamlet fund." Corson called this fishing "Marine style." He had best not try dynamiting fish in the presence of the peasants of rural America.

CHAPTER FOUR

The Lunarization Program

A joke circulating among Americans in South Vietnam is that a good final solution to the Vietnam problem would be to pave the country and make it a parking lot. This parking-lot vision is similar to the reality of American bases and Vietnamese refugee camps, with their uniform buildings arrayed in military precision on hot stripped land. The vision is also a cynically humorous recognition of the American war-machine's effects on the very earth of Indochina.

The nonliving, or abiotic, elements in ecosystems are inseparable from the plants and animals. Soil, temperature, solar and cosmic radiation, water, atmospheric gases, wind, and other environmental factors act in concert with the living organisms. Tampering with any element can touch off changes throughout the ecosystem.

A casual observer flying over Indochina can see that large expanses of its fields and forests have been pocked with craters. The craters are gouged by aerial bombardment, artillery shells, and rounds from warships. The 500- and 750-pound bombs in common use dig craters as large as 30 feet deep and 45 feet across. Statistics regarding the use of explosive ordnance in Indochina numb the senses; one must perhaps view the miles of countryside that have become lunar landscapes in order to realize the impact of saturation bombing on the land. Probably no district of South Vietnam is without its pitted fields or forests. Refugees from northeastern Laos report saturation bombing of the Plain of Jars and of all the valleys where land has been cleared for habitation and cultivation. Northern Cambodia and the Cambodian provinces bordering South Vietnam have also been bombed to support Cambodian troops and interdict enemy supplies. In the fall of 1970, the heaviest bombing of the Indochina war was carried out by B-52s against the Ho Chi Minh Trail area of Laos.

Craters have the obvious effect of making farmland useless for cultivation. I once saw a movie showing North Vietnamese peasants working only with hand tools to fill a huge bomb crater. The peoples of other Indochinese nations, even if they could be motivated to undertake such an endeavor, would be in grave danger of attracting further air attack. Also, South Vietnam and Laos have been bombed far more heavily than North Vietnam. B-52s have not been used against North Vietnam, because B-52s would be sitting ducks for surface-to-air missiles. So the North Vietnamese do not have to contend with the long swaths of craters those giant bombers create.

Another obvious land-defacement program is the denudation of roadsides and base perimeters by so-called Rome plows, which are huge bulldozers fitted with vegetation-stripping blades. Rome plows have also been used to level forests. Jonathan Schell described part of the plan of Operation Cedar Falls, an assault on the Iron Triangle:

> After the jungle had been heavily shelled and bombed, the 1st Division troops were to flatten the jungle in fifty-yard swaths on both sides of the road, using sixty bulldozers airlifted in by the huge, two-rotor Chinook helicopters. Then they were simultaneously to destroy the villages of Rach Bap, Bung Cong, and Rach Kien, evacuate the villagers, and start cutting broad avenues in the jungle with special sixty-ton bulldozers nicknamed hogjaws. These drives would be supported by air strikes and artillery barrages against the jungle.

Plows, explosives, and herbicides have combined to transform the abiotic elements in much of Indochina. The precise effects of these military tactics on the abiotic aspects of the environment are not known, because investigations have not yet been made. Clyde Wahrhaftig, Professor of Geology at the University of California in Berkeley, has suggested that current military activity is possibly affecting the soils of Indochina in five ways:

1) Irreversible hardening of lateritic soils to form laterite hardpans or crusts.
2) Gullying, sheetwash, landslides, and other forms of accelerated soil erosion on steep mountainous slopes with red and yellow podzolic soils and possibly also with non-calcic brown soils.
3) Disturbance of protective peat layers covering extremely acid and saline alluvial soils of the Ca Mau Peninsula.
4) Salt-water intrusion into rice-paddy fields.
5) Loss through leaching of the available nutrient supply of tropical forests growing on nutrient-poor soils.

Other observers have described three other ways in which current military activity possibly affects the abiotic elements of the environment. These ways are: (6) Watershed destruction, which causes changes in nutrient supplies to lowland rice fields, silting, increased flooding, and drought; (7) Local changes in climate; and (8) Destruction of soil microorganisms, which may be caused by changes in their soil habitat and by the toxic effects of herbicides.

The rest of this chapter is devoted to a discussion of each of these eight possibilities.

1) Lateritic soils are widespread in tropical areas where temperatures are high and rainfall abundant throughout the year. Silicas and other minerals are leached from lateritic soils by the constant downward movement of water, leaving the soils rich in iron oxide and alumina. Lateritic soils are widespread in Cambodia and the fertile plateaus of Laos. They account for about 30 percent of South Vietnam's soils.

The action of roots and the shading effect provided by leafy canopies, enable tropical forests to keep lateritic soils porous. However, if the forest is stripped away, these soils may harden into a brick-like crust. Crusting can occur within two years.

Blocks of laterite were used in constructing Angkor Wat, which is eight centuries old. A striking example of hardening of lateritic soil was described in the MRI Report:

> At Iata in the Amazon Basin, the land was deforested and bulldozed for an agricultural colony. What appeared to be a rich soil, with a promising cover of humus, disintegrated after the second planting. Under the equatorial sun, the iron-rich soil began to bake into brick. In less than five years the cleared fields became virtually pavements of rocks.

About four percent of the Mekong delta is underlain by lateritic soils. If the rice fields on these soils are not irrigated and silted regularly, they may become barren. Military tactics that craterize and strip the land not only force farmers to abandon their fields, but may also be paving portions of Indochina.

2) Large areas of the mountainous regions of Indochina are covered by podzolic soils, which have a high clay content and leached upper layers, and by non-calcic brown soils, which are sandier and occur in relatively dry areas. These soils are highly susceptible to accelerated erosion if the vegetation is removed from them. As Clyde Wahrhaftig has written, "Extensive and indiscriminate cratering by high-explosive bombs could have the same effect as a massive road-building program, in that it could lead to rapid gullying, landsliding, etc., which might ultimately lead to the exposure of unweathered bedrock, and would certainly lead to floods of silt and sand in valleys and on downstream watercourses."

The monsoon downpours of Indochina cause rapid erosion. Tschirley noted gully and sheet erosion where there was little or no vegetation, such as on the perimeters of military bases in South Vietnam.

3) The acidic and saline soils of the Rach Gia area on the western side of the Ca Mau peninsula are overlain with peat. These peaty soils can be intensively cultivated as long as the water level remains high. If the water level falls, the peat dries and burns readily. Deep bomb cratering also renders such

land unproductive because it destroys the protective peat cover and mixes the acidic subsoil with the peaty surface soil.

4) The destruction of mangrove forests, the Mekong delta's line of defense against the sea, permits bank erosion and salt-water intrusion into rice fields. The cratering of fields and dikes, coupled with forced abandonment of rice land, causes extensive erosion in terraced rice fields and permits the sea to reclaim portions of the delta.

5) In a tropical forest, most nutrients are in the living form of plants. Nutrients are rapidly recycled, and roots make up for nutrient loss by drawing upon the parent rock. If the trees are destroyed by herbicides or other means, runoff and infiltrating rainwater wash away the nutrients on which the forest had depended. It is this edaphic transformation, this impoverishment of the soil, which is the major factor in succession of tropical forest to savanna.

6) Precipitation throughout Indochina is characterized by the wide seasonal variation of the monsoon cycle. The amount of rainfall also varies greatly from year to year. Often, too much or too little rain falls during the crucial months of the cycle of rice cultivation. As a result, rice growers in Indochina have always had to contend with devastating floods and droughts.

Destruction of watershed forests can only make the rivers and estuaries of Indochina more inhospitable to human life. Both floods and droughts are worsened, silting of fields is increased, and the regular flow of nutrients is disturbed. During the fall of 1970, huge floods swept the valleys of coastal central Vietnam. This region, called in military jargon the I Corps region, is characterized by relatively short rivers flowing into coastal valleys. It has been heavily bombed, defoliated, and bulldozed. Residents of the I Corps region cannot exist above ground in many rural areas, let alone maintain or improve their dikes and irrigation works.

7) The great quantity of life (biomass) and of species diversity in a tropical forest depend partly on year-round high temperatures and heavy rainfall. Defoliation can destroy the microclimate of the forest, as we have seen. But the destruc-

tion of a forest by defoliation may also alter the macroclimate, the weather cycle that affects the whole ecosystem. As the MRI Report said, "If an ecosystem's vegetation is destroyed to such a degree that there is a resultant decrease in the evapotranspiration within that system, the macroclimate of that area may eventually be significantly altered."

The MRI Report noted that annual rainfall decreased on the deforested plains of Spain. The report also cited the results of a four-year study of the Tennessee's so-called Copper Basin, a 7,000-acre area that was denuded by fumes from a copper smelter. Compared with an adjoining forest, the denuded area had higher soil temperatures during the summer and greater temperature fluctuations throughout the year. During the growing season, soil temperatures 22 degrees (Fahrenheit) higher than in the forest area caused higher evaporation in the bare zone. Summer wind velocity was 13 times greater than in the forest. In any six-month period, rainfall was greater in the forest, although the researchers judged rainfall comparisons to be inconclusive.

8) Soil microorganisms are the chief decomposers of an ecosystem. Without decomposers, matter cannot be cycled through the living-energy system. Soil microorganisms break down plant and animal waste material and convert it into carbon dioxide, water, and plant nutrients. Decomposers improve soil fertility in three main ways: (a) ammonification, which is the conversion of proteins and other complex nitrogenous materials to ammonia; (b) nitrification, which is the conversion of ammonia to nitrate ions; and (c) nitrogen fixation, which is the conversion of atmospheric nitrogen to a form usable by plants. Microorganisms also play an important role in the detoxification of herbicides.

Changes in soil habitat, such as erosion or exposure to sunlight, certainly transform the nature of the soil's community of decomposers. I have seen no studies of this matter, but alterations in the microorganism community must have far-reaching consequences for the rest of an ecosystem.

The MRI Report cited findings about the auxin herbicides (2,4-D, 2,4,5-T, and picloram) that they had no toxic effect on some microorganisms, inhibited others, and increased the numbers of yet others. The effect of cacodylic acid on decomposers was not mentioned by the report.

Leguminous plants such as beans are important crops in Indochina, especially for the Montagnards. In these plants, nitrogen-fixing bacteria infect the roots to form nodules. Legumes are often used to enrich soil with nitrogen for the benefit of other crops. The MRI Report stated:

> The efficiency of nodulation of leguminous plants is reduced by 2,4-D and beans grown in soil treated with 2,4-D (both the first and second crops after 2,4-D treatment) had lowered protein contents but the reason is unknown. . . . 2,4-D appears to slow down the nodulation on soybean plants but this does not appear to present any practical problem since the bean plants themselves are exceedingly sensitive to the phenoxy herbicides, and it is unlikely that one would attempt to grow beans on fields freshly sprayed with these herbicides.

A Montagnard whose small bean field has just been sprayed with Agent Orange or White may not be reassured by this logic.

CHAPTER FIVE

Airs, Waters, and Places: Environments of Disease

Early one afternoon I was sitting in an open-air restaurant in a small South Vietnamese town, consuming a bowl of the wonderful noodle soup that is a specialty of that country. Suddenly the hostess frantically began covering exposed meats and the soup pot. A spray truck passed by, enveloping the restaurant, soup, and me in a heavy white mist of DDT. The DDT settled and I ate on. In many South Vietnamese towns and cities, the DDT spray truck was (and probably still is) as regular a daily feature as dusk and the firing of H&I artillery rounds. It illustrates the profligate use of dangerous chemicals in Indochina, as well as the desperate need to suppress disease microbes that proliferate in the environments of the war.

Some 2,500 years ago, Hippocrates (or his ghost-writers) collected medical wisdom under the heading "Airs, Waters, and Places." Modern medical science is slowly returning to the belief of the ancients that human disease is influenced by the total human environment. As Hippocrates wrote, the good physician is one:

> Who has a due regard to the seasons of the year, and the diseases which they produce; to the states of the wind peculiar to each country and the qualities of its waters; who marks carefully the localities of towns, and of the surrounding country, whether they are low or high, hot or cold, wet

or dry; who, moreover, takes note of the diet and regimen of the inhabitants, and in a word, of all the causes that may produce disorder in the animal economy.

The Second Indochina War is causing a tremendous physical and psychological uprooting of the Indochinese peoples. Hippocrates believed that "It is changes that are chiefly responsible for diseases, especially the greatest changes, the violent alterations both in the seasons and in other things. But seasons which come on gradually are the safest, as are gradual changes of regimen and temperature."

The wrenching changes occurring in Indochina are again showing that war and pestilence ride together. René Dubos has written of the disease-causing nature of population changes:

> A host of difficult medical problems have been created by the mass population movements so characteristic of our times—whether involuntary, as in the case of refugees, or voluntary, as in the case of pilgrims and persons who migrate to cities and other places of opportunity. These problems include infections caused by microbial agents acquired through new contacts with men or animals; the introduction of disease vectors; nutritional disturbances resulting from shortages in essential nutrients and even more from disturbances in food habits; and last but not least, the ill-defined but nevertheless severe sociocultural and psychic stresses always associated with life under new conditions.

An obvious medical effect of the war is the blowing-up, piercing, and incineration of people. No army in Indochina has a monopoly on ruthlessness; all are willing to crush noncombatants, women, and children in pursuit of their ends. The US Senate Refugee Subcommittee estimated that between 1965 and 1970 there were 1,000,000 civilian casualties of the war in South Vietnam, of whom 300,000 were killed. American firepower, used in application of the Devastation Model of counterinsurgency, without question produces more civilian casualties than any other force.

American ground-troop withdrawal does not mean that the maiming and killing of civilians is ending, because troop with-

ECOLOGY OF DEVASTATION: INDOCHINA

drawal is not an end to the war. The Refugee Subcommittee staff cited an American government report from Quang Tri province which noted that 18,414 "war victims" were produced in that province during a period of only one month, from May 21 to June 20, 1970. According to the staff:

> The report went on to predict a continued generation of war victims "at the comparatively high level of 10,000 per month." According to the report, "in Quang Tri most of the damage to houses and a substantial proportion of the deaths and injuries to civilians resulted from friendly action and stray fire from GVN and US forces." The report also indicates "that these losses were quite small in comparison with those sustained in the three southern provinces" of Quang Ngai, Quang Tin and Quang Nam (in I Corps).

Medical facilities in South Vietnam are abysmally poor. There are very few Vietnamese MDs and almost all of them are in the army. Doctors from the United States, Taiwan, and the Philippines staff the provincial hospitals, where they must deal with fear, staggering work loads, and Vietnamese workers who are often lazy and thieving. When asked by Refugee Subcommittee investigators what he needed most, the senior doctor at the Quang Ngai hospital replied, "To end the war—for as long as the war continues we will continue to run just to stand still in our efforts to provide better medical treatment for the Vietnamese."

War casualties are, of course, "generated" in all Indochinese nations. This account will not dwell on this obvious form of war-caused suffering. Rather, the toxic effect of sprays and gases tossed about Indochina will be discussed, with a look at US government control of toxicity information. A broad view of the effects of the war on human disease ecology in Indochina will be presented. To show the link of disease with psychological dislocation, a brief report on some refugees of the Raglai Montagnard tribe is offered.

Poisons from the Airs

There is a striking sentence tucked away without comment on page 190 of the MRI Report: "According to DiPalma (1965), a man committed suicide by consuming about 6.5 g of 2,4-D; from this and the other information, it appears that the lethal dose for a human lies in the range of 50 to 100 mg/kg." On page 152, the MRI Report noted that chemicals with an LD_{50} (dose lethal to 50 percent of test creatures) in amounts of 50 milligrams per kilogram (mg/kg) of body weight are classified as "highly toxic"! A few drops to one teaspoon of such chemicals will kill a 150-pound man. If the LD_{50} of a chemical is 50 to 500 mg/kg, the chemical is considered "moderately toxic," and it takes from one teaspoon to one ounce of it to kill a 150-pound man. By correlating spray rates presented on page 141 of the MRI Report with "milligrams per square foot" statistics on page 153, we find that the standard defoliating dose of Agent White (2,4-D and picloram) distributes about 150 milligrams per square foot, and that Agent Orange (2,4-D and 2,4,5-T) puts down about 250 milligrams per square foot. Then, on page 198, the dogged reader finds that 2,4,5-T is considered slightly *more* toxic to animals than 2,4-D!

If, as the Defense Department's MRI Report claims, 2,4-D is lethal to humans at 50 to 100 mg/kg, then even the severest critics of herbicides have underestimated the toxicity of 2,4-D. Below are some of the case histories found on pages 189–90 of the MRI Report, "presented here to permit the reader to form his own opinion about the magnitude of the hazard associated with the use of 2,4-D compounds."

> Goldstein et al. (1959) in their report on peripheral neuropathy after skin exposure to an ester of 2,4-D state that three individual patients, two farmers and a female bookkeeper, suffered the disorder some hours after exposure to the 2,4-D formulation while attempting to kill weeds. The symptoms progressed through a period of days until pain, paresthesia and paralysis were severe. Disability was protracted and recovery was incomplete even after a lapse of years. They concluded that there was little doubt that the

symptoms resulted from the percutaneous absorption of the 2,4-D. The electromyographic examinations supported the diagnosis of peripheral neuropathy. Berkley and Magee (1963) report a similar case of neuropathy in a 39 year old farmer four days after exposure to 2,4-D dimethylamine salt; the symptoms included numbness and incoordination of the hand and finger muscles and a slow recovery. These authors conclude that persons who get peripheral neuropathy from exposure to 2,4-D are very rare compared to the number of exposures there must be. They state that some individuals may have a predisposition to neuropathy and suggest that all users of these herbicides use protective clothing and wash immediately with soap and water in case of accidental exposure.

NLF figures of about 300,000 people poisoned per year from 1966 through 1969 by chemicals, mainly herbicides, may be close to the truth. Vietnamese adults generally weigh less than 150 pounds, the herbicides concentrate in such places as wells and cisterns, and small children cannot be kept from eating sprayed plants. Also, Vietnamese sprayed by agents White or Orange cannot "use protective clothing and wash immediately with soap and water." If I read the MRI Report correctly, 2,4-D is far more toxic to people than to the animals on which it has been tested.

Biologists, much less laymen, cannot be expected to read the MRI Report as if it was a jigsaw puzzle. Controversy about the toxicity of defoliants has centered around evidence that 2,4,5-T is highly teratogenic (fetus-deforming). The story of how this evidence came to light bears repeating.

Herbicides have been widely used in the United States since the early fifties. They have been sprayed over wide areas of Indochina in unprecedented concentrations since 1961. Nevertheless, neither the American government, industry, nor private scientists began comprehensive studies of the toxic effects of herbicides until after the 1962 publication of Rachel Carson's book, *Silent Spring*.

In 1964, the National Cancer Institute of the Health, Education, and Welfare Department (HEW) commissioned the

Bionetics Laboratory to test various widely-used pesticides and industrial compounds for carcinogenic and teratogenic effects on laboratory animals. By the summer of 1965, the Bionetics Laboratory had obtained results indicating that 2,4,5-T in small doses causes birth defects in mice. Late in 1966, Bionetics had completed a preliminary report on 2,4,5-T. Officials of the Food and Drug Administration (FDA) knew of this report by 1968, and officials of the Agriculture and Defense departments learned about it in 1969. No one else saw the Bionetics Report.

The National Cancer Institute released the Bionetics carcinogenicity findings in April 1969. Few noticed that the teratogenicity studies were withheld. In July, an employee of the FDA slipped a copy of data from the Bionetics Report to Anita Johnson of the Center for Study of Responsive Law, a group colloquially known as Nader's Raiders. The data showed that small doses of 2,4,5-T and slightly larger doses of 2,4-D cause birth defects in rats and mice.

Miss Johnson showed this data to Dr. Matthew S. Meselson of Harvard, who told Nader's Raiders of its significance. The Nader group met an official wall of silence about the report. Dr. Meselson was told that the final Bionetics Report was "classified and confidential." Meselson alerted Dr. Samuel Epstein, a member of an official HEW study commission on pesticides. After struggling for weeks with official resistance, Epstein finally got the Bionetics findings for inclusion in the commission's December 1969 report. A subsequent test on chick embryos performed by Dr. Jacqueline Verrett of the FDA indicated that 2,4,5-T, 2,4-D, and the mixture of their n-butyl esters that constitutes Agent Orange are all teratogenic in tiny doses.

In April 1970, largely because of the furor sparked by these disclosures, the Defense Department stopped using Agent Orange in Indochina (except for "mistakes" such as that discovered by Ronald Ridenhour, noted in Chapter 2). Agent White, with its 2,4-D, is still in use at this writing.

Why was the Bionetics Report concealed by officials of the departments of Defense, Agriculture, and Health, Education, and Welfare? A former White House staffer told the Nader group that disclosure of the report would have fueled the antiwar movement and fed international criticism of American chemical warfare. FDA officials cited pressure from chemical companies, especially Dow Chemical, as the main force keeping the truth from the public.

It is difficult even under the best circumstances to determine the effects of herbicides on people. Results of testing on animals may not apply to human beings. Cases are rare in which a specific malady in human beings, such as a birth defect, can be traced to a specific chemical. For example, 2,4,5-T often causes cleft palates in mice, and cleft palates are common human birth defects. It is easy to see that in the environment of the Indochina war, diseases are running rampant. But it is often impossible to trace or identify the causes of those diseases.

The Vietnamese people certainly believe that herbicides are harmful to people. "Defoliants are causing egg-bundle-like fetus catastrophe at Tan Hoi Hamlet," bannered the June 26, 1969 issue of the Saigon newspaper *Tin Sang*. Women of Tan Hoi, reported the paper, were flocking to Saigon hospitals "for having their egg-bundle-like fetuses or monsters taken out. . . . They unanimously say that after just about two months of being pregnant, their fetuses become unbearable to them; then blood starts coming out through their vulvas until the fetus is taken out or the unfortunate pregnant woman must die." The Thieu regime promptly shut down *Tin Sang* and also prevented private Vietnamese citizens from seeing the birth-defect records of Vietnamese hospitals.

Thomas Whiteside worked out a calculation based on the standard dose of Agent Orange applied to wells and cisterns in South Vietnam, which led him to conclude that "if a Vietnamese woman who was exposed to Agent Orange was pregnant, she might very well be absorbing into her system a percentage of 2,4,5-T only slightly less than the percentage that deformed one out of every three fetuses of the pregnant experimental rats."

The Herbicide Assessment Commission of the AAAS was particularly concerned with the possibility that 2,4,5-T was causing birth defects in South Vietnam. It reported in December 1970 that records of about 4,000 abnormal births in Saigon Children's Hospital from 1959 to 1968 show a sudden rise in two types of defect (cleft palate and spina bifida) after the start of heavy spraying in 1966.

The AAAS commission found that the rate of stillbirths in Tay Ninh provincial hospital was 64 per thousand, compared to 31.2 per thousand throughout South Vietnam. The Herbicide Assessment Commission's report noted, "Although, as in other areas where agent Orange has been used mainly for forest destruction (as opposed to crop destruction) the total number of directly exposed Vietnamese is probably low, the northern portion of Tay Ninh has been heavily defoliated and the rivers draining the areas of defoliants run through the remainder of the province and are a source of fish for some of the population."

A Defense Department study suggested that the rate of stillbirths in Vietnamese provincial hospitals had declined to 31.2 per thousand from a 1960–65 rate of 36.1 per thousand. Both the AAAS and Defense Department scientists noted that, without further study, their findings could not be related directly to the effects of herbicides.

AAAS investigators are also seeking to trace minute amounts of the deadly poison 2,3,6,7-tetrachlorodibenzo-p-dioxin, which is generally called dioxin. Dioxin is produced as a result of the manufacture of 2,4,5-T. It always contaminates the final 2,4,5-T product. It may be a product of the chemical breakdown of 2,4,5-T and possibly of 2,4-D as well (according to Dr. Jacqueline Verrett). Dr. Matthew S. Meselson of the AAAS team noted that one part per billion of dioxin will kill a guinea pig. Dioxin resists chemical decomposition and is soluble in fat, which means that it probably concentrates in animals and humans much as DDT does. Workers in 2,4,5-T plants in the US and West Germany have developed chloracne as a result of dioxin poisoning. It is a disease characterized by extensive skin eruptions, liver damage, disorders of the central nervous system, chronic fatigue, lassitude, and depression. Dr. Verrett has determined by tests on chick embryos that dioxin is a million times more potent a fetus-deforming agent than the notorious drug thalidomide.

The crop-killing Agent Blue is composed of cacodylic acid, an organic arsenical compound that becomes inorganic arsenic in the human body. Orians and Pfeiffer have written, "Symptoms of acute poisoning from cacodylic acid are headache, vomiting, diarrhea, dizziness, stupor convulsions, general paralysis, and death. The dosage required to cause these symptoms may be as little as one ounce (28 grams) of cacodylic acid per human adult." And a man committed suicide by taking a mere 6.5 grams of 2,4-D!

Herbicides are not the only poisons that have been distributed in the airs of Indochina. Dr. Arthur H. Westing of the AAAS study-team noted that more acres of South Vietnam had been sprayed with Malathion (to kill malaria-bearing mosquitoes) than had been sprayed with herbicides. Westing speculated that chickens reportedly killed by herbicides might actually have died of Malathion poisoning.

The extent and effects of Malathion spraying in Indochina are important subjects for future scientific investigation. According to Polly Roberts of the Center for Study of Responsive Law:

> Malathion belongs to the organophosphate family of insecticides, which includes the notorious parathion, responsible for over half the insecticide deaths in the United States. A single "large" dose of one of these chemicals, or a series of small doses over a period of several weeks, lowers the body level of the vital enzyme cholinesterase. When the level gets low enough the victim suffers cramps, vomiting, convulsions, and, without immediate treatment, death.
>
> Malathion has the peculiarity that it can be rapidly broken down by an enzyme in the liver of mammals; thus it has only a moderate toxicity of about 6,000 mg./kg. A person with a diseased liver, or one who has recently been exposed to other toxic chemicals, may succumb to much smaller doses. Considering the prevalence of diseases such

AIR, WATERS, AND PLACES: ENVIRONMENTS OF DISEASE

as liver flukes in Viet Nam, and the frequency of exposure to other toxic chemicals such as DDT and the herbicides, a sizable fraction of the population may be quite susceptible to malathion.

The tear gases known as CS and CN, as well as the nausea gas called DM, are often used in South Vietnam to drive people out of tunnels and bunkers so they can be captured, incinerated, or chopped up by other weapons. These gases, according to two MDs of Harvard, "are incapacitating, but usually non-lethal, although they can kill under certain circumstances: extremely high concentration of agent or highly susceptible victim, such as the very young, the very old or the very sick." Dr. Alje Vennema of Ontario, while serving in the Quang Ngai provincial hospital in 1967, treated a number of patients who had been exposed to canisters of gas (probably DM) while hiding in bunkers. Dr. Vennema wrote, "Patients are feverish, semi-comatose, severely short of breath, vomit, are restless and irritable. . . . The mortality rate in adults is about 10 percent while the mortality rate in children is about 90 percent."

In 1966, US aircraft dropped 12 tons of CS on a jungle near the Cambodian border. Masked American troops charged into the cloud, but found no trace of any enemy. I was sitting in a remote district outpost in 1968 when the American district adviser, a major, returned from a conference with his superiors. The major had been urged to use more CS gas. He was considering spreading CS on an area believed to be used by the NLF as an infiltration route. A captain on his team explained that CS would only make the guerrillas uncomfortable. I noted that since the VC (as we called them) blame all ills on American poisons, the CS would be grist for enemy propaganda mills. The major decided not to use the CS.

Stagnant Waters and Unhealthy Places

The effects of environments created by the Indochina war on human health are even more mysterious than are the other ecological effects of the war. Americans, like worshippers of the Greek drug deity Panacea, tend to regard the expansion of medical facilities as a sign of increased health. Even if doctors and hospitals were profuse in Indochina, which they are not, disease would run rampant among the Indochinese. There is no panacea for people living in environments favorable to disease. Restoration of physical and social health depends on a change in the environments. It also depends on the slow adaptation of human beings to their new ecological circumstances.

Writing about Saigon in 1966, Frances FitzGerald summed up health conditions in South Vietnam—conditions that have continued to deteriorate:

> Given its topography and a climate like that of New York or Washington in a perpetual summer, Saigon will never be a healthy city. Given the overcrowding, the lack of drainage, of sewage and garbage collection, it may rate as one of the least healthy cities in the world. According to the Doxiades study of 1963, not less than 10 percent of persons ten years and older has clinically significant pulmonary tuberculosis. The infant mortality rate of 36.2 percent is significantly higher in Saigon than in any other region of the country. Despite the massive inoculation program initiated by USAID and the World Health Organization, cholera, smallpox, and bubonic plague, as well as leprosy and typhoid, have become endemic to almost every population center of Vietnam, owing to the movement of refugees.
>
> The diseases for which there are no vaccines—malaria, amoebic dysentery, eczema, worms, and an unspecific sort of swamp fever—will continue to kill people until living conditions show some improvement.

The complexity of environmental effects on disease may be illustrated by focusing on malaria. Malaria is a term for a series of diseases, all of them caused by microbial parasites and transmitted when certain types of mosquitoes bite an infected human or animal and then bite a new victim. The incidence and severity of malaria can be affected by ecological changes in the habitats of mosquitoes, in the human and animal carriers, and in the malaria parasite itself.

In Indochina, the highland valleys have been the environment of the most extensive and virulent forms of malaria. In the Mekong delta, malaria has not been widespread, because the mosquitoes that act as malaria vectors (carriers)—*Anopheles philippinesis*, *A. aconitus*, and *A. culicifacies*—have existed there in relatively low densities.

Owing to saturation bombing, great expanses of craters have been formed in the lowlands of Indochina. These craters fill with water and may remain swampy even during the dry season, when the fields and canals are empty. Like the craters, the stagnant channels of urban slums are excellent breeding places for mosquitoes acting as malaria vectors.

The various ethnic groups of Indochina are adapted to living at quite specific elevations. Over a period of centuries, the Indochinese have also adapted to the forms of malaria endemic to their habitats. By becoming urban refugees, the Indochinese concentrate the human hosts needed by malaria microbes. The people are also exposed to malarial forms for which they have no defenses. For example, Tom Xerii of International Voluntary Services, Laos, reported that of 1,900 Meos resettled from their mountain habitat to a highland valley, 140 soon died from severe malaria attacks and malnutrition.

The spread of malaria in Indochina is analogous to a situation described by Dubos:

> There are good reasons to believe, for example, that malaria, and consequently the sickle-cell anemia associated with hemoglobin S, became prevalent in Africa as a result of the slash-and-burn agriculture that created stagnant pools favorable for the breeding of *Anopheles gambiae* larvae. More generally, the spread of primitive agriculture into potentially malarious areas brought man in contact with insects and built populations of sufficient density to maintain a reservoir of infection.

The American and South Vietnamese governments respond to the creation of malarial environments by spraying insecticides. Malathion has been sprayed more extensively than herbicides in South Vietnam, probably killing chickens, honeybees, and people. DDT has been sprayed in towns and cities, getting in my and other people's soup. The insecticides strike with ham-fist at the environment, disrupting natural balances and possibly creating conditions hospitable to diseases far worse than malaria. John P. Milton of the Conservation Foundation cited a report from a northern Thailand town indicating that DDT had killed all the cats and had consequently caused an explosive increase in the rat population!

Dubos wrote, "Populations of insects, like populations of microbial parasites and of all other living things, rapidly give rise to mutant forms possessing genetic resistance to the poisons with which they come into contact." Malaria-bearing mosquitoes also develop behavior patterns, which protect them from insecticides. Mosquitoes have been known to begin resting outdoors after houses have been sprayed with DDT and to adopt what is called excito-repellency behavior. "The effect of excito-repellency," explained Dubos, "is that the insect concerned avoids lethal contact with the insecticide; but this does not reduce its attacks on man, and so transmission of the pathogen continues."

As insects mutate to resist insecticides, the malaria microbes mutate to resist anti-malaria drugs administered to patients. *Plasmodium falciparum* is a particularly virulent malarial parasite, which often invades the capillary system of the brain by way of the red blood cells. It blocks the flow of oxygen and causes brain damage or death. Milton noted, "The development, particularly in *P. falciparum*, of varieties resistant to chloroquine and mepacrine cures has added to problems with malaria in SE Asia. Only quinine or a combination of sulfurmethoxine and diaprim remains an effective cure in such cases."

Americans, of course, have generally not developed resistance to any forms of malaria. US troops in Vietnam are usually required to regularly take so-called malaria pills, which they are told will protect them from catching malaria. The doctor advising my International Voluntary Services program advised us not to take malaria pills, because many doctors believe these pills merely suppress the symptoms of malaria. People often show signs of having malaria after discontinuing

AIR, WATERS, AND PLACES: ENVIRONMENTS OF DISEASE

pill use. At least the pills keep American troops out there fighting, whether or not they have malaria.

According to Milton, other water-related diseases (diseases needing water for the survival of the microbial parasite or its vector) prevalent in Indochina include schistosomiasis, opisthorchiasis (liver fluke), paragonimiasis, cholera, typhoid, keptospirosis, amoebiasis, hemorrhagic fever, and filariasis. The same factors that are increasing the danger of malaria may also be making these diseases more deadly to Indochinese peoples. A full-scale ecological analysis of all major diseases of Indochina could be of great benefit to the people there.

Diseases show even less respect than armies for national boundaries. Strains of microbial disease that can cause epidemics anywhere may spread throughout the world. Bubonic plague, for example, has persisted in Asia. Environmental conditions and human adaptation have prevented plague from doing to Asians what it did to Europeans in the Middle Ages. Plague is carried by fleas, which in turn ride on rats and other animals. Conditions in urban South Vietnam are hospitable to rats and offer plenty of weakened humans for infestation by the plague microbe.

In 1961, eight cases of plague were reported in South Vietnam. By 1965, there were an estimated 4,500 plague victims. The World Health Organization reported in 1968 that plague had reached "epidemic proportions" in South Vietnam, causing 330 deaths and over 5,000 illnesses in less than eleven months of 1967.

Americans, and many people living in zones controlled by the South Vietnamese Government, receive inoculations against plague. The cause of the plague epidemic is environmental and the possibility of development of plague strains resistant to vaccine is great. The US Public Health Service sent 550 workers to South Vietnam in 1966, to make sure no rats climbed on planes bound for America.

It is a matter of common knowledge and great concern to Americans in Vietnam that horrible types of venereal disease are circulating in local whorehouses. Some of these forms of

VD are collectively and colloquially termed the black syph, because they are highly resistant to medication. There is no way to confine the black syph to Indochina.

In November 1970, the American Social Health Association declared that, in America, venereal disease is now a pandemic, meaning an epidemic of unusual extent and severity, occurring over a wide area and affecting a very high proportion of the population. In the year ending June 1970, infectious syphilis recorded a sudden increase in America, after a six-year decrease in incidence. Venereal disease pandemics have been declared only twice before in America—at the end of World War I and toward the end of World War II—and were presumably associated with the return of troops from overseas. The American Social Health Association attributed the present pandemic to the sexual revolution in America. It is also true that hundreds of thousands of US troops are rotated in and out of South Vietnam, all of whom are on one-year tours of duty.

The Last of the Raglai

The Raglai, whose name means "men of the forest," are Montagnards traditionally living in the upper river valleys on the southeastern rim of the Annam Cordillera. Numbering a few thousand in population, the Raglai speak a Malayo-Polynesian language similar to the language of the Chams. They are farmers of upland rice and swidden vegetable crops, and gatherers of bamboo and other wild mountain plants for trade with lowland peoples.

In the hills surrounding the valley in central coastal Vietnam where I lived from early 1967 to early 1969, there were three Montagnard villages consisting of two Raglai villages and one K'ho village. During the mid-sixties the NLF established base camps near those villages. Red lines on American and South Vietnamese government maps marked off the Montagnard homeland as a free-strike zone, where anything moving was fair game for troops and aircraft. The Montagnards were forced to move to a resettlement camp located on a bare, stark plain just outside the lowland town nearest the mountains. As a community development volunteer, I set out to improve the living conditions of these 1,500 dispossessed people.

The refugees had no land to farm. All arable land was already being cultivated by Vietnamese, Chams, and Nung Chinese living in the valley. The war prevented opening new land to cultivation. The bolder Montagnards braved NLF kidnapping and US-GVN military operations to farm mountainside plots and to cut bamboo for sale to Vietnamese merchants. Some worked as field hands and livestock watchers for lowlanders. Their main income source was the pitifully inadequate salaries paid to soldiers. While local Vietnamese struggled to avoid military service because they could make more money as civilians, 14-year-old Montagnard boys enlisted in the militia and in cadre programs so their families could survive.

Refugees were entitled to six monthly allotments of bulgur wheat and salad oil, after which they were taken off the rolls and pronounced "resettled." Refugee supplies were controlled by the Vietnamese refugee service. The Montagnards were also supposed to receive a cash sum. However, the provincial refugee service chief decided he should use the money to buy rice for the refugees, because Montagnards were simple savages who would otherwise spend the money on alcohol. The chief stole much of the money and rice, as well as all other refugee relief items. He refused to transport what goods remained from the provincial warehouse to the refugee camp. Americans had almost no control over what this Vietnamese chief did with aid supplied by the US. I spent many frustrating weeks talking US military men into flying and convoying refugee supplies to the Montagnards.

Disease took a heavy toll among the Montagnards. I helped to save some lives by arranging medical evacuation by helicopter to the provincial hospital. Many more died in their huts of unknown causes. Dysentery complicated by malnutrition was probably the most frequent killer. The Montagnards rarely sought modern medical attention. They would make ceremonies to the spirits. If the patient's health continued to decline they preferred to let the person die at home, where his spirit could be put to rest. Once a First Cavalry doctor arrived and had a few patients flown to the provincial hospital, where they were successfully treated. One woman, however, had horrible open wounds covering her legs. This case baffled the doctor, who shook his head, took her picture, and left.

Militarily, the refugee villages were suspended between the defensive perimeter of the lowland town and the NLF-controlled hills. They lived in constant fear that either the NLF would come down and kill them or US-GVN forces would wipe out their homes in reaction to an attack launched through their villages. The NLF threatened them when they went to the mountains for wood and bamboo. By late 1968, most people in two of the three refugee villages had moved into lowland towns for further protection. Montagnard troops, many of them mere children, were rapidly killed in the flash battles regularly gnawing at the GVN outposts in the valley.

I helped a dedicated group of lowland Cham schoolteachers in their efforts to establish a primary school for the Montagnards. Many Montagnards realized that the school system was a way of integrating their children with the lowland culture, so prevented their children from attending. They had no place, economically or culturally, in the valley, and wanted only to go back to their highland villages. I could list many reasons for the failure of my development projects, but the underlying cause was the Montagnards' concept of the refugee camp as a place to wait for death.

The Montagnards see the Vietnamese much as the American Indians viewed the nineteenth-century whites. NLF troops were simply called *Yuan glai* ("Vietnamese of the forest"). Stoically the Montagnards would wind through the streets of the lowland towns, walking single file as though on a jungle path. Montagnards who had recently fled the mountains stood out among their fellows, because their faces lacked the dull glaze of spiritual resignation. Always the Montagnards asked me to get America to fight the Vietnamese, a race they believed to be executing their genocide.

AIR, WATERS, AND PLACES: ENVIRONMENTS OF DISEASE

Similar brief pictures of physical and cultural decay could be drawn about refugees of all the ethnic groups of Indochina. Without the war maintained by American men and arms, cultural conflict in Indochina would be severe; with the war, cultural conflict is genocidal. In South Vietnam, Laos, and now Cambodia, peoples are forced to experience war in environments that can no longer sustain their lives.

CHAPTER SIX

Environments of Technocratic War

At the Conference on War and National Responsibility held during February 1970 in Washington, D.C., Professor Arthur W. Galston of Yale University proposed that an international agreement ban "Ecocide: the willful destruction of the environment."

The term ecocide began appearing in literature about the Second Indochina War soon after the widespread application of herbicides became known. Genocide, a word coined by jurist Raphael Lemkin between the two world wars, refers to intentional assaults by a government against the people of a whole culture, race, or communal group. Genocide was defined at the 1948 Geneva Convention by reference to what Nazi Germany had done to the Jewish people. Ecocide is a concept that probably will be defined by an international group in the near future, possibly at the United Nations conference on the environment scheduled for 1972 in Stockholm. It is a concept that will be modeled on what the United States Government is doing to Indochina.

Ecocide as an act of war, to essay a definition, is the intentional destruction of large portions of the natural and/or man-made environment that serves to sustain human health and life.

In these terms, American actions in Indochina are ecocidal. Destruction by US men and machines of the environment that supports human life in Indochina has been, and continues to be, massive. Environmental annihilation is intentional. It is the expressed will of US government organizations, in applying what I have called the Devastation Model of counterinsurgency, to deprive so-called insurgents of the people, land, food, shelter, medical facilities, oxygen, and other environmental elements that are necessary for life.

From the point of view of the power that wages ecocidal war, the most important characteristic of ecocide is that it is self-defeating. The political loyalty of people cannot be gained by a power that is destroying their environment. A devastated ecosystem cannot be economically exploited. Populations cut off from the environments in which they make their livings cannot produce wealth. Ecocide is good policy only for those who can thrive, economically and spiritually, in an environment of perpetual war, which draws the lifeblood from all societies involved.

The devastation being wrought in the Second Indochina War lashes back at America. American men die, the US economy is drained, national resources and attention are diverted from fighting social decay at home. The war gives power to forces within the government that are willing to lay waste to environments in order to seek short-term political gains. Plant and animal species that could enrich life in America are threatened with extinction. Diseases are spawned in Indochina for importation into the United States.

Peoples of other nations have come to view America as an insanely dangerous power. The US Government has often claimed that it must fight communism in Indochina or be forced to fight communism elsewhere; the sad truth is that the Indochinese war is so costly, physically and psychologically, that America's ability to support its allies elsewhere is greatly reduced.

For America, in my opinion, the greatest cost of the Indochina war is paid by the emotions and intellects of individual citizens. I know the confusion and brutalization that can occur to a young man sent to fight in Indochina. Americans construct much of their self-identities from their images of

America. The reader may judge for himself whether US actions in Indochina fill him with pride or with a sense of lingering guilt.

None of these statements are new. Now, the Nixon administration assures us, America's Indochina adventure is ending. Troops are being withdrawn and it is said that by mid-1972 there no longer will be US troops in combat in Indochina. The Special Forces no longer command little tribal armies in South Vietnam. Herbicides, after wreaking widespread destruction to little or no purpose are, according to the Pentagon, being phased out. Journalists of all schools write of the Indochina war in the past tense, sifting the ashes for political lessons. Most Americans want to believe that the war is over and want to let Indochina sink back into the obscurity where it rested a decade ago.

Unfortunately, US troop withdrawal is not an end to the Indochina war. The desperate governments, tribes, and communal groups that America supports in Indochina will fight on. North Vietnam and its friends and allies will continue their struggle.

Troop withdrawal is not even an end to *American* involvement in Indochina. The cruel irony is that without US ground troops in Indochina, American destruction of peoples and environments will probably increase. The crushing might of technology has always been used there in order to "save American lives." With US troops gone, the engines of destruction must be deployed more massively in order to maintain the American position in South Vietnam, Laos, and Cambodia. Each escalation of devastation—the invasion of Cambodia, the saturation bombing of the Ho Chi Minh Trail area of Laos, the renewed bombing forays over North Vietnam—has been justified by saying that it saves American lives. It is a vicious cycle that only strengthens enemies of the US Government.

Few denouncers of the Indochina war are willing to say precisely how America can get out of it. The only way out at this point is to negotiate withdrawal *on the enemy's terms*. In other words, to escape a war it never declared, the US Government must surrender. America must surrender more than a war. It must abandon the counterinsurgents' mechanistic view of Indochinese peoples and environments. The US Government does not seem willing to do that; like an inept poker player, it throws good blood and treasure after bad, hoping its enemies will fold out of the game.

But the cards are already on the table. War critics are proven correct with every ugly story emerging from Indochina. Why, then, does the war continue? An editorial in *The New Yorker* offered this opinion:

> Perhaps one reason is that the gap between the official explanations and the realities we are faced with daily on television and in the newspapers has become so staggeringly huge and so obvious that when one persists in making these points one feels almost ludicrously simple-minded. . . . It is as though the public had shrugged its shoulders and decided to accept the war as something that cannot be affected by human effort. The war has outlived the *issue* of the war . . . the actual conduct of the war is developing according to a completely separate set of rules, determined by the conditions of unspeakable brutality and confusion in Vietnam itself.

"The war has outlived the *issue* of the war." To which may be added that the effects of the war, as well as the human structures created to wage it, will outlive the war itself. For human society, like Nature, adapts and evolves in response to changing environmental conditions. The Second Indochina War may be viewed as an event in the process of social evolution. An ecological perspective is useful in assessing the effects of the war. A similar perspective may be employed to analyze the social systems driving the US Government to continue it.

Biological theories should be applied to human society only with great caution and qualification. In the nineteenth century, misinterpretation of the biological writings of Charles Darwin led to the philosophy of social Darwinism. As René Dubos has explained:

Herbert Spencer and the social Darwinists saw in the theory of evolution a mechanism—supposedly ethical because it was presumed to be based on natural laws—that accounted for the survival of the fittest. In their view, this mechanism explained and justified continued prosperity for the upper social classes. The weeding out of the weak members of animal populations in nature appeared to some Victorians a sufficient excuse for imperialism, sweatshops, child labour, and slums.

The social Darwinists held that political and economic progress was best served by applying to human affairs the competitive and destructive practices they assumed to constitute the law of the jungle. This simplistic approach had no scientific justification. Darwin himself rejected the view that organic evolution based on selection of the most vigorous forms depended exclusively on competitive and destructive practices in nature. He had clearly stated that "in numberless animal societies, struggle is replaced by cooperation."

Social Darwinism is not without its latter-day advocates. But as the science of ecology emphasizes the interdependence of all life forms, social science now recognizes the interdependence of social institutions. These new perspectives are interconnected. Dubos has observed, "Scientific interest in the cooperative aspects of animal life increased in the Western world precisely at the time when social mores began to condemn imperialism and social injustice."

The American military structure that carries on the Indochina war may be viewed as an evolving feature of American society. Just as though it were a mutating organism, it is shaped by society and, in turn, causes society to adapt to it. It draws its energy from the American public and thrives in a peculiar environment of ideas.

Mankind's anatomical evolution—the development of the structure and size of the human body and brain—was apparently completed 50,000 years ago. Changes in human society are attributable to cultural rather than biological evolution. The responsibility and hope of human life are implicit in Dubos' identification of the difference between cultural and biological evolution:

> Changes mediated through genetic mechanisms are usually slow in manifesting themselves, but are lasting, and in many cases seemingly almost irreversible. In contrast, changes mediated through psychosocial mechanisms correspond to a Lamarckian type of evolution: the knowledge and skills acquired by one generation are transmitted directly to the next but persist only as long as conditions remain favourable for their direct transfer; what is gained through their agency in one generation can be completely lost in the next.

As the psychosocial mutations created by one generation can be lost by the next, so they can be discarded by an act of will. Mankind, to borrow a metaphor developed by ecologist F. R. Fosberg, shows signs of being a pioneer species. "The pioneer," wrote Fosberg, "exerts a strong effect on its environment and tends to change it relatively rapidly, soon rendering it unsuitable for its own further occupancy." Humanity, however, could culturally evolve to become a climax species, "which lives in such adjustment with its environment that it is able to occupy it relatively permanently without serious modification." Through an assertion of the informed human spirit, the Earth can remain habitable by our species. We may well begin by halting the ecocidal war in Indochina, a goal which cannot be achieved without understanding the technocratic structure that wages the war.

Technocracy at War

The Second Indochina War has brought to prominence a number of social philosophers who, in their various ways, describe the "military-industrial complex" and sometimes the whole American system as a machine run amok. Americans are told that they live in the New Industrial State, the Corporate State, the Megamachine, and similarly unsavory social environments. Novelist Norman Mailer has described bureaucracies growing like cancer. The fantasies of William S. Burroughs present the body politic as a terminal junk addict.

I propose to add to this spate of theories by focusing on what I have seen and read of the Second Indochina War. The American structure that carries on the war is best described as a technocracy. Technocracy may be defined as a uniting of bureaucratic organization with modern scientific technology.

Bureaucratic organization combines a hierarchical chain of command with specialization of function. Like a feudal chieftain, the head of a bureaucracy issues directives, which flow down through its lower levels. But because of specialization the bureaucratic administrator does not know precisely what orders to issue. The specialist, because of his exclusive knowledge, becomes powerful and independent. The specialist controls bureaucratic information. A bureaucracy cannot be tightly controlled from the top. Indeed, it cannot be controlled from any one quarter.

When specialists are sent by a bureaucracy to work among the various tribes and factions of Indochina, central control is virtually lost. The specialists can and do create communal armies without anyone in Washington knowing just what is going on. The situation is complicated because bureaucrats and bureaucracies in the form of private contractors, quasi-governmental organizations (such as Air America), military services, intelligence organizations, and civilian government agencies swarm around Indochina, often working at cross-purposes.

Interbureaucratic strife in Laos has been particularly well documented. To cite a recent case, I spoke with a man who worked with the AID outpost in Sam Thong during 1969. The CIA was set up in nearby Long Cheng, where it supplied and advised Vang Pao's Clandestine Army. As the former AID man told it, the AID contingent wanted to pull the Meo tribe out of its suicidal fighting role, by flying the whole tribe to northern Thailand if necessary. On the other hand, the local CIA command was pushing to fight communism to the last Meo. A CIA-advised squad set up a mortar position above Sam Thong and the AID boys were afraid (groundlessly, it seems) that the CIA was going to mortar them!

Bureaucracies, like organisms, struggle to survive. There

is now a large number of American Indochina-war professionals inhabiting Indochina and Washington. Drifting among various government agencies and private contractors, these men are at home in the environment of the war. Like me, many young Americans have spent a number of post-college years becoming proficient in some aspect of the so-called Indochina programs. In Laos, a miniature American colonial society has developed, complete with a second generation being raised in Vientiane. Indochina-war professionals generally live in fear that their bureaucracies will fold out from under them. So their reports tend to claim that the light has been sighted at the end of the tunnel and that the corner has just been turned.

Bureaucracies and their various branches not merely strive to survive but also to grow. For example, the NLF has a shadow government for South Vietnam. There is also a shadowy parallel government in South Vietnam composed of US advisers. The country is divided into 44 provinces, each of which is subdivided into districts. Between 1967 and 1969 the American advisory population in the sub-province where I worked grew from about seven to forty or fifty. Security deteriorated steadily during that period. More Americans were sent there after I left.

In the provincial capital there was a hotel full of US Army advisers, a villa of Civil Operations Revolutionary Development Support (CORDS) advisers, a house of CIA advisers, and sundry mysterious American advisers wandering around, not to mention the American battalion stationed at the nearby airport. All of these advisory units grew steadily. At the time I left, they were laying plans for a large compound to house them all. Except for the CIA, which controlled its funds at the provincial level, these advisers had very little control over the South Vietnamese they were advising.

In order to grow, a bureaucracy must consume resources. It must also give the impression of producing results. The American bureaucracies of Indochina have developed ways to quantify all resources consumed and all results produced. Though the psychology of troop withdrawal is now probably having its effect, while I was in Vietnam there was constant command pressure to produce and consume ever more. Career advancements were believed to depend on increasing the numbers and amounts of rounds expended, bodies counted, hearts and minds won, money distributed, latrines built, bombs dropped, gallons of herbicides sprayed, pigs stied, and environmental features destroyed. Broadcast spraying of herbicides and saturation bombing of countrysides is largely a result of this terrifyingly simple bureaucratic growth-drive.

Seymour Melman has described the growth dynamics of not just the Indochina war programs, but of the whole Department of Defense. The Defense Department budget, Melman has noted, grew from $45 billion in 1960 to $83 billion in 1970. The Pentagon now consumes 10 percent of the Gross National Product of the United States. Melman observes that this expansion occurred mainly because "the state-management [Defense Department] shows a propensity in problem-solving to select solutions that also serve to extend its decision-power."

Some high-level Defense and State Department dropouts have recently been helping Senator William Proxmire depict the Pentagon as a careening nexus of bureaucracies. Townsend Hoopes, formerly Undersecretary of the Air Force, has described the Joint Strategic Operating Plan produced annually by the Joint Chiefs of Staff (JCS):

> In 1965–67 period [it] was one of those examples of military logic carried to ludicrous extremes. It presumed to establish the desirable size and composition of the military forces of nearly every sovereign non-Communist nation of the world; it calculated the military budget of each country, and then estimated the added equipment, training, and incremental funding that would be required to bring that country's armed forces up to JCS standards of size and quality.
>
> This annex [plan] was forwarded each year to the Secretary of Defense as JCS guidance for the development of the military assistance program; it included countries to which the U.S. neither gave nor contemplated giving military assistance.

Nicholas Katzenbach, Undersecretary of State in the last years of the Johnson administration, told Proxmire's subcommittee that he was "shocked" to learn that the Food-for-Peace program had generated about $690 million in weapons for third-world governments. Katzenbach also testified that he did not know that weapons had flowed to Greece for one or two months after April 1967, when Washington announced that arms shipments to Greece had ceased. But Katzenbach had been the man in charge of that program.

When bureaucracy mutates into technocracy by grafting on modern technology, it becomes overwhelmingly difficult to maintain human control. The specialists are further empowered by the mysteries of technical science. Costs rise astronomically. Expensive weapons-systems designed ten or twenty years ago suddenly emerge as metal-and-wire engines of death that cry out to be used.

Mankind cannot yet comprehend, much less control, the scope of technocratic war. Can one really envision the three million tons of high explosives dropped on the two Vietnams by 1969? What about the one million-plus rounds of H&I fire slung randomly into the darkness of South Vietnam in the course of a single year? Or try to envision the saturation bombing of northern Laos, which commenced immediately after the heavy bombing of North Vietnam ceased. To borrow an image from the Yellow-Peril threat-mongers, when one war program is snuffed out ten rush forward to take its place.

The GI inside the war is in a milieu to which mankind has not yet adapted. He rides in the tube of the C-130 troop transport, bombarded with metallic screeches and unable to see outside. On R&R (Rest-and-Recreation) he is likely to end up in Bangkok's Thai Heaven, where a Thai rock-group will hit him with driving electronic yawps. Only William S. Burroughs has captured the American Indochina-war environment:

> "Do not be alarmed citizens of Annexia—Report to your Nearie Pro Station for chlorophyll processing—We are converting to vegetable state—Emergency measure to

counter the heavy metal peril—Go to your 'Nearie'—You will meet a cool, competent person who will dope out all your fears in photosynthesis—Calling all citizens of Annexia—Report to Green Sign for processing."

"Citizens of Gravity we are converting all out to Heavy Metal. Carbonic Plague of the Vegetable People threatens our Heavy Metal State. Report to your nearest Plating Station. It's fun to be plated," says this well-known radio and TV personality who is now engraved forever in gags of metal. "Do not believe the calumny that our metal fallout will turn the planet into a slag heap. And in any case, is that worse than a compost heap? Heavy Metal is our program and we are prepared to sink through it. . . ."

Energy Sources

The Indochina-war technocracy consumes money, the produce of the planet, and the time of men. It draws these resources from the American people. The technocracy depletes one subcontinent in order to lay waste to another. If the energy sources of the war machine were cut off, America's role in the Indochina war would end.

World War II pulled America out of the Great Depression. The war made jobs and jobholders earned money. They spent this money, thereby creating more jobs for workers who would spend money, and so on. Economists call this phenomenon the multiplier effect.

The belief persists in America that even if the economy does not need war, it at least needs massive military spending. For example, cutbacks in certain Defense Department programs have called forth banner headlines about aerospace workers being laid off and cities consequently slipping into the economic doldrums. At the same time, Americans can feel the whole economy sinking and can observe a wide range of problems tearing at the social fabric. When one has actually seen the awesome waste of the Indochina war, it is difficult to believe that any economy could be made healthy by spewing its resources at Asia.

The truth is that war, because it is wasteful spending, can only stimulate the American economy in a time of heavy unemployment. As economist Robert Eisner has written, "Major escalation of our military role in Southeast Asia, beginning in 1965, took place against the backdrop of an economy near full employment. Resources for war mainly had to come not from idle capacity but at the expense of non-war production." After studying the Indochina war's effects on the American economy up until mid-1970, Eisner decided:

> The American economy as a whole is worse off by at least the more than $100 billion estimated to have been spent thus far in connection with our operations in Indochina. That some individuals have enjoyed "war profits," whether as investors, defense contractors, workers producing war material, or black market operators in Saigon, cannot obscure the total picture. If the economy as a whole has lost $100 billion, the arithmetic requirement that the whole equal the sum of its parts means that if some have gained, say, $50 billion, others must have lost $150 billion: $-100 = +50-150$. . . .
>
> The war has caused inflation. The war has caused high taxes. The war has contributed to housing shortages. The war has drained resources in the areas of education, transportation, housing and all the services of the government, from police protection to postal delivery. And the war and consequent inflation and government efforts to combat that inflation have now brought on the greatest stock-market crash since the thirties, the highest interest rates since the Civil War, falling production and rising unemployment.

Eisner noted that the average weekly spendable earnings of industrial workers with three dependents dropped 1 or 2 percent between 1965 and 1970, after having risen more than 11 percent between 1960 and 1965. He also quoted Louis B. Lundborg, chairman of the board of the Bank of America, as saying, "During the four years prior to the escalation of the conflict in Vietnam, corporate profits after taxes rose 71.0 percent. From 1966 through 1969 corporate profits after taxes rose only 9.2 percent." By Eisner's own calculations, corporate profits fell 11 percent between 1965 and the first quarter of 1970. Adding in hidden costs, such as man-hours lost in

Indochina, Eisner put the total cost of the war by mid-1970 at $212.9 billion.

After the Cambodian invasion, Wall Street moguls descended on Washington to argue against the war. As the war grinds on, it becomes increasingly apparent to more and more Americans that the conflict is hurting us all. The war is a crisis of American capitalism, not an economic stimulus. So we must end it before it precipitates a full-scale economic crash.

Looking at the total Defense Department system, Seymour Melman wrote, "To the older pattern of exploitative imperialism abroad, there is now added an institutional network that is parasitic at home. This combination is the new imperialism." The American system may, as Melman has suggested, be economically exploiting other nations. But, as he has also made clear, Indochina offers little opportunity for American capitalism. The Marxist view that the Indochina war is being fought to gain control of resources and to create new markets is nonsensical in light of both the war's drain on the American economy and its devastating effect on Indochinese economies.

The energy sources of the war technocracy differ from those of private capitalism. Melman has noted that "instability in costs, prices, and profits are not major constraints for the managers of the state machine." The Pentagon draws its fresh capital from American taxpayers through Congressional appropriations. Therefore it need not make a profit. In fact, as Melman has cogently argued, even the defense industries need not make a profit in the traditional sense of the word. Companies such as Lockheed and General Dynamics pile up phenomenal cost overruns on Defense Department contracts and are then kept from bankruptcy by Pentagon bonuses. For such companies, wrote Melman, "what is actually a bonus to the submanagement is called 'profit.'"

It costs the Defense Department about $400,000 to kill one person in Indochina. If America gets out of the war, the Pentagon assures us, other pressing defense needs will absorb the roughly $30 billion a year we have been spending on it.

ENVIRONMENTS OF TECHNOCRATIC WAR

America expends men as well as money on the war. The Defense Department's list of American Vietnam war casualties for the period from January 1, 1961 through January 2, 1970 reads as follows: 44,241 killed by hostile forces, 293,529 wounded nonfatally, 462 currently captured or interned, and 9,064 dead as a result of illness or other non-hostile action. (In addition, during the same period, the South Vietnamese armed forces lost 119,451 killed, the other so-called free-world forces lost 4,255, and the "enemy" lost 691,881. "Enemy" body counts often include civilian casualties.)

Americans do not like their fellow citizens to die in futile wars. So they place a disproportionately high value on American lives, which is noticed by all Indochinese. American war supporters cite this blood investment as a reason to continue the fight. With the help of the mass media, the President and the Defense Secretary focus on the plight of Americans held prisoner as a reason to attack North Vietnam.

Still, few Americans want to die in a lost war in order to save the face of their government or to buy time for withdrawal. Before the elections in the fall of 1970, President Nixon proposed a standstill cease-fire in South Vietnam. War critics hailed the proposal. The NLF scornfully rejected it. In fact, as news reports were hinting at the time, a situation similar to a de facto cease-fire was already in effect in South Vietnam.

The structure of the US ground forces in Indochina is rapidly rotting. Military discipline and morale were at a peak in South Vietnam when Americans were on the attack, in the heat of battle. Now American forces are static, with all the social mutations of American society being fed into them. By early 1969, when I left Vietnam, one could see morale crumbling, antiwar sentiment rising, black-power movements growing, and drug use increasing. Since then, the word "fragging" has entered the GI's jargon, to describe the frequent killing of unpopular officers by their own troops. Troop riots, only a few of which make the news in the United States, are becoming more common on American bases in Indochina.

ECOLOGY OF DEVASTATION: INDOCHINA

Officers often must cajole, rather than order, troops into the field.

The war no longer can be fought with large numbers of American draftees. The war technocracy has lost one of its major energy sources. Troop withdrawal may be regarded as the Defense Department's adjustment to the decay of its drafted forces. The draft is an unjust system, which has called for disproportionately large numbers of poor people and blacks to die for the United States. But it now appears that the draft may be replaced by an even uglier military system in Indochina. Under such a system, professional US troops, together with mercenaries and the forces of client military regimes, may wage a war similar to the classic colonial campaigns of the past and to the Portuguese colonial operations of the present. However, if the North Vietnamese and their Indochinese allies continue, as they probably will, to oppose the American presence, the United States will have to use its devastating weaponry to crush even more of the Indochinese peoples and environments.

The United States continues to be able to fight the Second Indochina War only through the compliance of millions of civilian taxpayers and military time-servers. The war technocracy's manpower resources are drying up and its funds can be cut off too. The war system thrives in a certain environment of ideas, but if these ideas are transformed the system may no longer be able to exist.

The Spectrum of Threats

"The first requirement we faced upon assuming office," Defense Secretary Melvin Laird said early in 1970, "was to reappraise the spectrum of threats that exist in the world today."

The Defense Department is able to wage war and to obtain appropriations for arms only in an environment of threats. It spends a lot of the taxpayers' money to define these threats for the American public. As of February 1969, for example, the Pentagon was spending about $4 million a year for 339 lobbyists, which averages out to one lobbyist for every two members of Congress.

Threats sell. Samuel F. Downer, financial vice-president of the LTV Aerospace Corporation, explained why he thought the post-Indochina-war "world must be bolstered with military orders":

> It's basic. Its selling appeal is defense of the home. This is one of the greatest appeals the politicians have to adjusting the system. If you're President and you need a control factor in the economy, and you need to sell this factor, you can't sell Harlem and Watts but you can sell self-preservation, a new environment. We're going to increase defense budgets as long as those bastards in Russia are ahead of us. The American people understand this.

Is America buying defense against a spectrum of threats or is it being sold on a specter of threats? We already have the nuclear capability to destroy the population of the Soviet Union between 400 and 600 times over. Does an overkill factor of, say, 1,000 provide any better defense than an overkill factor of one? Or is the arms race itself such a great threat to humanity that defense cannot be measured in terms of nuclear capability?

But the Defense Department is not really arming to defend. Rather, it is arming *to deter*. That, in turn, raises another pair of unanswerable questions: do ever-growing stocks of arms actually deter war or do they make apocalyptic nuclear conflict more likely? Even our participation in the Second Indochina War is often justified as an act of deterrence: if we don't fight "them" there now, we'll have to fight them somewhere else later.

Kenneth E. Boulding, an economist and ecologist, has written of the way that new ideas gain force in human societies:

> If we think of knowledge as a species, we see that this also grows, in part, by simple accumulation—that is, the addition of more items than are subtracted in a given period, as, for instance, the simple growth of vocabulary in a lan-

guage. There is also, however, a phenomenon that looks very much like mutation. This is the reorganization of knowledge into a new system, a new theory, a new way of looking at things, or even a new ideology. This happens usually in a single mind, from which, however, it can be propagated rapidly through a whole society if it happens to fit the particular ecological system of ideas which is prevailing at the moment. The spread of the growth of knowledge therefore seems to follow many of the principles of ecology, and the various kinds of knowledge flourish or decline according to the competition of other kinds of knowledge and according to the general habitat in which they are found.

The system of ideas concerning America's defense needs is rapidly mutating. Spurred by public criticism, Congress is beginning to reassert and use its constitutional powers in order to limit defense spending. However, it still has to overcome a long tradition of uncritical acceptance of Defense Department judgments. Representative Richard D. McCarthy has noted that "only a handful of members of the 435-member House of Representatives and the 100-member Senate, perhaps 5 percent, are thoroughly familiar with what is going on in the CBW area. Only five House Appropriations Committee members are cleared for 'top secret.'" McCarthy added that he had been told by a senior colleague in 1968 that not even the then House Majority Leader, Carl Albert, knew the identities of the five Appropriations Committee members familiar with the funding of the CIA, Green Berets, chemical and biological warfare (CBW), and other secret programs.

There is nothing inherent in the American political system that demands that a parasitic "deterrence" machine be financed at the expense of social health. No inexorable force drives America forward to repeated defeat in Indochina. The funding of the Pentagon can be cut back; it can even be reallocated to the solution of America's true social problems.

The Defense Department increasingly looks homeward for threats. Army intelligence agents have been assigned to report on antiwar groups and civil rights movements. Terrorist bombings serve the war technocracy by dramatizing threat. The urban guerrillas who want to reshape America and the self-styled patriots who support increased military buildup are ideological allies involved in an unacknowledged conspiracy to increase the power of the Defense Department.

On a worldwide scale, there exists a very real threat that modern technocracies, rather than just military technocracies, will waste the Earth in pursuit of short-term ends. An ecological perspective on the Second Indochina War exposes that war as a futile effort to render environments uninhabitable in order to save them from communism. In the decades ahead, we will also need to apply a similar ecological perspective to other problems of modern life.

In December 1970, the governing body of the American Association for the Advancement of Science approved Dr. E. W. Pfeiffer's resolution for an immediate halt to all herbicide spraying in Indochina. Now, perhaps, the American scientific community, together with the American public, will broaden its concern to encompass the total effects of the American military on the human ecology of both Indochina and the United States. The Defense Department has commissioned the National Academy of Sciences to undertake a study of the ecological effects of the war. This study should be paralleled by field observations of private scientists from many disciplines. The Pentagon already has a Director of Chemical and Nuclear Operations. To deal with the real spectrum of threats, it should also have a Director of Ecological Caveats.

CHAPTER SEVEN

Switchboard Devastation

It is time to look at the future environments of Indochina and see how they will be shaped by the war. This vision is based on a projection of current trends. However, I hope that my predictions are incorrect and that my stating them here will help transmute them into specters to be exorcised by the actions of the American people.

American military men, like the rest of us, are struggling to understand and cope with a technological world full of danger. In the bureaucratic jungle of the Pentagon, ideas appear and materialize into programs and organizations. Some programs die a lingering death owing to fund and manpower shortages. Other concepts flourish and become dominant policy. Ward Just, who has written well of this process, has observed:

> The Army is an institution of adversaries, and the prejudice of the branch carries straight to the top—a "general officer" is that in name only. But the general staff has apparently made its choice, and it is probably no accident that the choice is one in which all branches will share. It is STANO—surveillance, target acquisition, and night observation. More broadly, it is what Westmoreland once called "the automated battlefield," and its premises proceed directly from the Vietnam experience.

The idea of STANO, Just was told, is to *functionalize the threat*. General William C. Westmoreland has explained it much better than I could:

On the battlefield of the future, enemy forces will be located, tracked, and targeted almost instantaneously through the use of data links, computer assisted intelligence evaluation, and automated fire control. With first round kill probabilities approaching certainty, and with surveillance devices that can continually track the enemy, the need for large forces to fix the opposition physically will be less important.

Continuing in the tone of Dr. Martin Luther King's famous "I have a dream" address, Westmoreland said:

> I see battlefields or combat areas that are under 24 hour real or near real time surveillance of all types.
>
> I see battlefields on which we can destroy anything we locate through instant communications and the almost instantaneous application of highly lethal firepower.
>
> I see a continuing need for highly mobile combat forces to assist in fixing and destroying the enemy.
>
> The changed battlefield will dictate that the supporting logistics systems also undergo change.
>
> I see the forward end of the logistics system with mobility equal to the supported force.
>
> I see the elimination of many intermediate support echelons and the use of inventory-in-motion techniques.
>
> I see some Army forces supported by air—in some ininstances directly from bases here in the continental United States. . . .
>
> With cooperative effort, no more than 10 years should separate us from the automated battlefield.

This is the automated battlefield: a countryside seeded with sensors and bomblets, swept with radar and infrared spotlights and laser beams; artillery rounds, air strikes, and naval fire crashing down on blips and rustles monitored by electronic surveillance; and field troops pushing buttons and pulling switches as they fulfill their specialized roles as automatic data processors and information storers and retrievers. The killers are physically and emotionally separated from the killed. The system is backed up by C-5A jet transports, each of which can fly 600 field-dressed soldiers to short runways anywhere in the world.

ECOLOGY OF DEVASTATION: INDOCHINA

Indochina is presently being converted into an automated battlefield. US ground forces will be down to 250,000 men by mid-1971. Further swift reductions can be expected, owing to the decay of discipline in the ranks and to waning public support for US involvement. The Indochinese peoples have been coagulated into population concentrations. There they must stay, for the automated battlefield can be created only in an environment of broad no-man's-lands.

A crucial theater of future switchboard battle is the I Corps region, which consists of the five northern provinces of South Vietnam. There, local resistance to the French, Americans, and South Vietnamese Government has always been strong. The countryside, never rich, has been devastated. Mines and unexploded bombs, features of rural areas throughout South Vietnam, make an explosive environment of I Corps. People are jammed into cities, where they live what American refugee officials term a nonviable existence. Full-scale anti-American rioting broke out in the cities during the fall of 1970. Furthermore, the region's valleys were swept by floods.

The ultimate solution to the I Corps problem has been found, according to Franklin Stewart, who is the director of the aptly-named War Victims Program in South Vietnam. The US Government plans to finance the compulsory relocation of farming families who have been driven to the cities of I Corps. American officials estimate that between 200,000 and one million people will be moved; the South Vietnamese Government anticipates shifting between two million and three million people over a three-year period. "We expect that this year's allotted refugee fund will be exhausted during the first two months of the program," said Stewart early in 1971. "After that we hope to get additional money from the US government."

These people are to be moved to the Mekong delta and to the environs of Saigon. What awaits them there in the way of a new and better life? The reader is referred back to chapters 1 and 2 for a second look at the crowded and conflict-torn environments into which these people will be thrust. The

SWITCHBOARD DEVASTATION

concept of Vietnamese as humanoids—as pawns in a war game—is far from dead.

As this goes to press, the massive relocation program has been quietly shelved.

But the prospects of the I Corps solution can be said to be tactically dazzling: South Vietnam with a *permanently depopulated northern zone!* Then the real military might of America can be brought to bear. As Westmoreland said, "In Vietnam where artillery and tactical air forces inflict over two-thirds of enemy casualties, firepower is responsive as never before. It can rain destruction anywhere on the battlefield within minutes . . . whether friendly troops are present or not."

Responsive firepower and the metallic rain of destruction proceed directly from the implementation of the STANO concept. However, the Defense Department is being very, very quiet about its electronic surveillance programs. Nevertheless, there are a few small holes in the department's veil of secrecy. For example, the *New York Times* reported on February 13, 1970: "The Pentagon is studying a proposal to provide enough modern sensing devices so that South Vietnam could seal its entire 900 mile border against sizable enemy infiltration." In the same month, an article in *Air Force and Space Digest* announced the installation of Seek Data II in Saigon. Seek Data II is a computerized system to swiftly relate intelligence data to air strikes. At Nakhorn Phanom Air Force base in Thailand, there is apparently a system called Project Alpha, which monitors sensors along the Ho Chi Minh Trail and along the Laos-Thailand border.

It is commonly known that sensors have long been in operation as part of the McNamara Line just below the Demilitarized Zone. But other surveillance programs are also coming to light. In October 1970, for example, the *Los Angeles Times* ran a remarkable story by George McArthur, who had visited a Special Forces radar site in the Mekong delta. The Green Berets, wrote McArthur, were monitoring sound and magnetic sensors, radar, infrared searchlights called "Flashy," and other devices. The main Delta Line of electronic surveillance ran about 50 miles, from Chau Doc to the Gulf of Thailand, with thinner monitoring to the north.

McArthur found that the Special Forces site was in contact with the Naval Operations Center, which, through Operation Dufflebag, had electronic probes in Cambodian territory that were more extensive than those in Vietnam. Low-flying aircraft swept the Cambodian countryside nightly to pick up signals from the devices below. Blips spotted and rustles heard called forth swift artillery and air strikes.

In December 1970, a top-secret B-57 bomber was shot down in Laos. About 20 B-57s had begun operating out of Ubon Air Base in Thailand in October. These airplanes, in addition to their bombs, rockets, cannons, and machine guns, are fitted with electronic sensors and radar. They are designed for night surveillance and attack.

The automated battlefield in the Indochinese countryside is already being supplemented by tight police control in the cities. As police advisers proliferate, the efforts to "root out the enemy infrastructure" expand. As the war grinds on and the influx of American money slows, the cities of South Vietnam become socially explosive.

Meanwhile, the American civilian advisory program has entered a holding phase. No one speaks any longer about winning the hearts and minds of the Indochinese people. Southern Illinois University (SIU) has been granted $1,000,000 by the Agency for International Development (AID) for "Strengthening within Southern Illinois University Competency in Vietnamese Studies and Programs Related to the Economic and Social Development of Vietnam and Its Post-War Reconstruction." The head of AID, John A. Hannah, explained to Senator Fulbright that the SIU center would "produce technical and professional personnel for assistance as requested in the post-war economic and social reconstruction of Vietnam—with particular attention being paid to Vietnamese and American veterans of the Vietnam conflict for such service."

Postwar reconstruction is the new—and rather premature —civilian catchword. The SIU center is designed to maintain a pool of Vietnam "other war" professionals and to train compliant South Vietnamese. Strong student and faculty opposition has emerged at SIU, and it may prevent establishment of this administrative training academy.

As this writing is completed (February 1971), large South Vietnamese army operations are underway in eastern Cambodia and the Boloven plateau of southern Laos. The invading troops work in the eye of an inferno of American air strikes, which are ravaging the rubber plantations of Cambodia and the coffee, spice, and other crops grown on farmlands of the Boloven plateau.

Communist forces have resisted these invasions. They also have launched sharp attacks against Vang Pao's CIA-advised Clandestine Army in northern Laos. A new level of Indochinese absurdity was reached when the US Air Force accidentally bombed Long Cheng, headquarters of the Clandestine Army. Because many of Vang Pao's loyal Meos are now dead, this army has been heavily reinforced with Thai mercenaries. The Royal Laotian Government's position is now so dismal that Premier Souvanna Phouma, who never objected publicly to the saturation bombing of the fertile areas of the Laotian highlands, has called for the withdrawal of South Vietnamese troops from Laos.

At best, South Vietnamese incursions into Cambodia and Laos will cause short-term disruption of communist forces and supply lines. When the South Vietnamese withdraw, as they eventually must, the history of their thrusts will be written on the landscape. The governments in Pnom Penh and Vientiane will continue to totter along as American dependents, unless the communists choose to use their forces to wipe those governments out.

The US has resumed bombing of North Vietnamese missile and radar sites. Emboldened by evidence that the US Government is determined to pursue what it sees as victory in Indochina, South Vietnamese President Thieu has said that "a march to the north is only a matter of time." The North Vietnamese, with their whole population trained in military arts, are amply prepared to meet such an invasion.

ECOLOGY OF DEVASTATION: INDOCHINA

President Thieu has metaphorically explained the wisdom of carrying the hot fighting outside of the borders of South Vietnam: "When we fight pirates outside our house only our mango and guava trees are damaged. But when we fight them inside the house, how can we keep the furniture from being destroyed?" Much of South Vietnam's furniture is already splintered. Anti-American, antiwar, and anti-government organizations continue to grow in South Vietnam's cities. The NLF is intensively working to turn these forces to its ends.

How will "the enemy" respond to the automated battlefield? North Vietnam seems to be economizing on force, turning more of its young people to tasks of rebuilding bombed structures, and pushing for rapid industrialization.

Indochinese communist thinking emphasizes long, phased organizing efforts, culminating in a general strike to sweep the revolution into power. The 1968 Tet offensive was an attempt to mobilize the South Vietnamese people into driving out the US-GVN forces with one swift blow. A similar attempt probably will be made again when the NLF and North Vietnamese think that the Americans are sufficiently weak and the South Vietnamese people psychologically prepared. What will the American government do if this happens? The possibilities stagger the imagination.

In 1955, Richard Nixon, then Vice President, said:

> It is foolish to talk about the possibility that the weapons which might be used in the event war breaks out in the Pacific would be limited to the conventional Korean and World War II types of explosives. Our forces could not fight an effective war in the Pacific with those types of explosives if they wanted to. Tactical atomic explosives are now conventional and will be used against the military targets of any aggressive force.

The nuclear weapons are now out there, ready to be used. By one estimate, as of 1968, the US had more than 5,500 nuclear weapons in Southeast Asia. Most of them were on aircraft carriers. Can nuclear devices be used in counterinsurgency warfare? Hanson Baldwin, the former military editor of the *New York Times*, has supplied one answer:

> On the other hand, the careful and precise use of an atomic shell, fired from an 8-inch howitzer, the utilization of atomic land mines to guard a frontier (as now proposed by Turkey), the creation of a restricted and carefully controlled radioactive belt in virtually uninhabited country through which any aid from outside the country would have to pass, or the use of atomic demolition devices in thick jungle areas or in precipitous defiles to cause tangled "blow-downs" or landslides to block trails, roads or natural approach routes could substitute for manpower and add great power to the defense.

Daniel Lang's recent interviews of US officials and of thinkers who ponder the unthinkable indicate that these and many more uses of "nukes" are certainly being considered in an Indochinese context. So far the horror of Hiroshima and the fear of cataclysmic consequences have prevented their use. But *if*—and I believe I should add *when*—America's dwindling forces in South Vietnam face a massive military assault while entangled among hate-filled civilians and a South Vietnamese Army that feels betrayed, the President may decide to unleash atomic weapons. If he does, as former Secretary of State Dean Rusk told Lang, "It would destroy not only the answers but the questions. It might be our last political decision."

There is still time for the United States to agree with the North Vietnamese and National Liberation Front that all of its men *and* machines should be withdrawn from Indochina. It would be an ugly surrender, a loss of territory and of worldviews, an abandonment of Indochinese who by force or choice have staked their destinies on continuing American presence. It would also be an act of political courage probably unprecedented in American history. It would be a bold recognition of the consequences of pursuing the Indochina war to a final denouement.

The Second Indochina War is certain to end. The US Government will pick up its troops and weapons, its advisers and sensors, and come back home. The question is: how many more tactics and weapons will be applied to Indochina, how many more years of devastation must the environments of Indochina suffer, before America relinquishes its grip on the fate of the Indochinese? This question will be answered, in part, by the resistance of the Indochinese people. The rest of the answer will come from the American people, who have a greater stake in what their government does to the ecology of Indochina than they may realize.

Notes

Introduction

A concise and environmentally sensitive view of the Khmer empire is offered in Christopher Pym, *The Ancient Civilization of Angkor* (New York: The New American Library, 1968).

Chapter 1: Fractured Spirit, Tempered Blade

Human ecology is discussed by F. Fraser Darling, "The Ecological Approach to the Social Sciences," in Paul Shepard and Daniel McKinley (eds.), *The Subversive Science* (Boston: Houghton Mifflin, 1969), pp. 316–27.

Mountain Tribes and Valley Kingdoms

The cultural history of Indochina is summarized in Charles F. Keyes, "Peoples of Indochina," in *Natural History* (October 1970), pp. 41 ff. The basic ethnic study of Indochina is Frank M. LeBar, Gerald C. Hickey, and John K. Musgrave, *Ethnic Groups of Mainland Southeast Asia* (New Haven: Human Relations Area Files Press, 1964).

For a study of the ecology of swidden agriculture and paddy cultivation, see Clifford Geertz, "Two Types of Ecosystems" in Andrew P. Vayda (ed.), *Environment and Cultural Behavior* (New York: The Natural History Press, 1969), pp. 3–28. Agricultural conditions under the French are described in M. Y. Nuttonson, *The Physical Environment and Agriculture of South Vietnam, Laos and Cambodia* (Washington, D.C.: American Institute of Crop Ecology, 1963).

The history of the First Indochina War and its cultural effects is drawn mainly from Bernard Fall, *The Two Viet-Nams* (New

York: Praeger, 1964). The figures on the extent of *agrovilles* are from Robert Scigliano, *South Vietnam: Nation Under Stress* (Boston: Houghton Mifflin, 1964), p. 105. An account of the Montagnard involvement in the Second Indochina War up to 1966 is found in Bernard Fall, *Viet-Nam Witness* (New York: Praeger, 1966), pp. 190–96. For obvious reasons Indochinese population estimates are very rough.

Michael Morrow's Burmese revelations appeared in the *San Francisco Chronicle*, October 16, 1970, p. 22.

South Vietnam: Draining the Insurging Seas

The "bring the people to the government" quotation is from "Refugee and Civilian War Casualty Problems in Indochina: A Staff Report," Subcommittee to Investigate Problems Connected with Refugees and Escapees, of the Committee on the Judiciary, United States Senate (September 28, 1970), p. 24. (Hereafter this is referred to as "Refugee Problems in Indochina.")

The basic study of Vietnamese village culture is Gerald Cannon Hickey, *Village in Vietnam* (New Haven: Yale University Press, 1964). Refugee movement from North Vietnam is discussed by Bernard Fall in *The Two Viet-Nams*, pp. 153–54.

The early history of American pacification efforts in South Vietnam is found in William A. Nighswonger, *Rural Pacification in Vietnam* (New York: Praeger, 1966), pp. 34–70. A full discussion of the Philippine Model of counterinsurgency is given in Napoleon D. Valeriano and Charles T. R. Bohannan, *Counter-guerrilla Operations: The Philippine Experience* (New York: Praeger, 1962). An account of the Malayan Model and its application in Vietnam is Sir Robert Thompson, *Defeating Communist Insurgency* (New York: Praeger, 1966). For a concise critique of so-called counterinsurgency models, see Bernard Fall, *The Two Viet-Nams*, pp. 337–84.

No one is likely to excel the description of American military tactics in Vietnam found in Jonathan Schell, *The Military Half* (New York: Random House, 1968). Refugee statistics are from "Refugee Problems in Indochina," p. 3, which also contains a discussion of the reclassification program. The 1968 population estimates and the Saigon population figures are from Samuel P. Huntington, "The Bases of Accommodation," in *Foreign Affairs* (July 1968), p. 648. The estimates for Qui Nhon, Da Nang, and An Khe are by American provincial workers.

Dr. Hannah's testimony is in "Civilian Casualty, Social Welfare and Refugee Problems in South Vietnam," Subcommittee to Investigate Problems Connected with Refugees and Escapees, of the Committee of the Judiciary, United States Senate, 91st Congress, First Session, Part 1 (June 24–25, 1969), pp. 5–10. (Hereafter this is referred to as "Refugee Problems in South Vietnam.") The testimony of subcommittee investigators regarding Operation Russell Beach is on page 46 of the same document, as well as on page 50 of "Refugee Problems in Indochina." On page 49 of "Refugee Problems in South Vietnam" is the investigators' report on the Cam Ranh hamlets.

The quotation from Dr. Huntington is on page 652 of his article, "The Bases of Accommodation."

Laos: The Subterranean Environment

The account of Meo history is summarized from Frank M. LeBar, et al., *Ethnic Groups of Mainland Southeast Asia*, pp. 63–81. Laotian Meo population figures are from "Refugee Problems in Indochina."

A full account of the making of the Clandestine Army is Don A. Schanche, *Mister Pop* (New York: David McKay, 1970). Vientiane political tangles are unraveled by Hugh Toye, *Laos: Buffer State or Battleground* (New York: Oxford University Press, 1968). More recent events and interpretations are found in Nina S. Adams and Alfred W. McCoy (eds.), *Laos: War and Revolution* (New York: Harper & Row, 1970). Opium culture is discussed in the same book in an article by David Feingold, "Opium and Politics in Laos," pp. 322–39.

The history of recent war activity and refugee movement in Laos is drawn from "Refugee Problems in Indochina," pp. 17–34. A translation of Jacques Decornoy's article, "Laos: The Forgotten War," appears in *The Bulletin of Concerned Asian Scholars*, vol. 2, no. 3 (summer 1970), pp. 21–33. Meos in Thailand are described by Arnold Abrams in *Far Eastern Economic Review* (*FEER*) (July 2, 1970), pp. 20–22.

Edgar Buell's "running and dying" statement appeared in *Life* (April 3, 1970). His estimate of Meos with the Pathet Lao is from the *Washington Post* (March 4, 1970). (These and other news reports are reprinted in "Refugee Problems in Indochina.")

Fred Branfman's findings are from his letter of March 17, 1970 to Senator J. W. Fulbright. The old man's description of "fire bombs" and the note about making paraffin lamps from cluster bomblets, are reported in the *Manchester Guardian* (March 14, 1970).

Cambodia: FARK versus FUNK

An account of Sihanouk's ouster is T. D. Allman, "Anatomy of a Coup," *FEER* (April 9, 1970), pp. 17–22. The Khmer Loeu rebellion is described by T. D. Allman in *FEER* (February 5, 1970), pp. 23–25. The Khmer Rouge is covered in *FEER* (September 4, 1969), p. 11.

A good background on Cambodia and its ethnic groups is provided by David J. Steinberg, *Cambodia* (New Haven: Human Relations Area Files Press, 1959). The fact that Sihanouk allowed Vietnamese settlers into Cambodia is noted in *FEER* (April 23, 1970), p. 16.

Refugee movement since the fall of Sihanouk is described in "Refugee Problems in Indochina," pp. 35–40. The population and ethnic composition of Pnom Penh is from T. D. Allman, "Change Comes to Pnom Penh," in the *This World* section of the *San Francisco Examiner & Chronicle* (September 20, 1970), p. 26.

Economic conditions in Cambodia are described in *FEER* (July 16, 1970), pp. 32–33; and in *FEER* (August 6, 1970), pp. 16–17. See *FEER* (November 7, 1970), pp. 23–26, on the US and ARVN presence in Cambodia. The growth of Lon Nol's army and military operations in Cambodia are reported in *Newsweek* (October 12, 1970), p. 57; and in *Newsweek* (November 9, 1970), p. 46. The Cambodia aid program was covered in the *New York Times* (December 28, 1970), p. 53. A visit by T. D. Allman to a Thai training camp on the Cambodian border is reported in *FEER* (August 6, 1970), p. 13. Richard Dudman's account appeared in the *New York Times* (June 24, 1970).

Saigon: Fractured Spirit

The Saigon city budget figure is from Frances FitzGerald, "The Tragedy of Saigon," in Barry Weisberg (ed.), *Ecocide in Indochina* (San Francisco: Canfield Press, 1970), p. 146. Estimates of political prisoners are from Michael Morrow in the *San Francisco Chronicle* (November 5, 1970), p. 21. The study of Xom Chua is noted by Professor Huntington in "The Bases of Accommodation," p. 649.

Figures on South Vietnam's economy are from Stephen Enke, " 'Vietnamizing' Vietnam's Economy," in the *Wall Street Jour-*

nal (October 5, 1970); in *FEER* (July 2, 1970), p. 61; in *FEER* (July 16, 1970), pp. 22–27; and the report of Associated Press correspondents Fred S. Hoffman and Hugh A. Mulligan published in the *Oakland Tribune* on October 21 and 23, 1970. The currency-smuggling ring is mentioned in Noam Chomsky, *At War With Asia* (New York: Random House, 1970), p. 71.

A summary of the Joint Development Group report is *Postwar Development of Viet-Nam* (Washington, D.C.: Embassy of Vietnam, 1969); The quotation is from page 70.

Robert Jay Lifton's perceptive discussion of Vietnamese and American psychology in Saigon, "The Circle of Deception—Notes on Vietnam," is in Barry Weisberg (ed.), *Ecocide in Indochina*, pp. 169–83.

Senator Nghiem's letter is quoted in Robert Shaplen, "Letter From Indo-China," *The New Yorker* (May 16, 1970). Professor Trung's statement is from Noam Chomsky, *At War With Asia*, pp. 65–66.

The CIA estimate of communists in the GVN is from the *San Francisco Chronicle* (October 19, 1970), p. 14. Ngo Cong Duc's statement is in *The New York Review of Books* (November 5, 1970), pp. 18–22.

North Vietnam: Tempered Blade

An account of land reform in North Vietnam is in Bernard Fall, *The Two Viet-Nams*, pp. 152–68. The quotation from Fall is from pages 152–53.

The best report of recent conditions in North Vietnam is Gérard Chaliand, *The Peasants of North Vietnam* (Baltimore: Penguin, 1969). On pages 38–46 of that volume is a summary of agricultural development. The quotations of Chaliand are from pages 120–21.

For a view of bombing damage, see John Gerassi, *North Vietnam: A Documentary* (New York: Bobbs-Merrill, 1968). A comprehensive tour by a long-time Hanoi supporter is described in Wilfred G. Burchett, *Vietnam North* (New York: International Publishers, 1966).

Chapter 2: The Green Devolution

Concepts of ecosystems and trophic levels are explained in W. D. Billings, *Plants, Man, and the Ecosystem* (Belmont, Calif.: Wadsworth, 1970), pp. 4–6.

ECOLOGY OF DEVASTATION: INDOCHINA

Attempts to create fire storms are described in Thomas Whiteside, *Defoliation* (New York: Ballantine/Friends of the Earth, 1970), pp. 50–51.

The Midwest Research Institute's report, *Assessment of Ecological Effects of Extensive or Repeated Use of Herbicides* (AD 824 314, 1967), is available from the Clearinghouse for Federal Scientific and Technical Information, Springfield, Virginia 22151. Quotations of the MRI Report are from pages 3, 258, and 263.

Matthew S. Meselson's quoted statement was given in the *International Herald Tribune* (September 14, 1970), p. 4. The Joint Development Group's summary report, *Postwar Development of Viet-Nam*, is quoted from page 22 regarding the income of South Vietnamese farmers.

Operation Ranch Hand (Hades)

The history of the development of herbicides and their military use in Indochina is told in the MRI Report, pp. 5–7 and 108–18; and in "A Technology Assessment of the Vietnam Defoliant Matter," Report to Subcommittee on Science, Research and Development, of the Committee of Science and Astronautics, US House of Representatives, 93rd Congress (August 8, 1969), pp. 2–19 (hereafter called "A Technology Assessment"). F. J. Delmore's quoted statement is from the MRI Report, p. 111; herbicide targets are listed on pp. 124–25.

Overall estimates of areas sprayed with herbicides are from "Background Material Relevant to Presentations at the 1970 Annual Meeting of the AAAS," which is the unpublished preliminary report of the Herbicide Assessment Commission for the American Association for the Advancement of Science, December 1970 (hereafter called the Herbicide Assessment Commission Report).

The range of herbicide drift is mentioned in A. W. Galston, "Defoliants," in Steven Rose (ed.), *Chemical and Biological Warfare* (Boston: Beacon, 1969), p. 63.

Frank Harvey's visit to Ranch Hand headquarters is covered in his volume, *Air War—Vietnam* (New York: Bantam, 1967), pp. 39–43. The code name "Operation Hades" was mentioned by Thomas Whiteside, *Defoliation*, p. 8. The suspension of use of Agent Orange was reported in the *San Francisco Chronicle* (June 23, 1970) and given the lie by Ronald Ridenhour in *Time* (November 2, 1970), pp. 39–40. The "phase-out" of all herbicide operations was reported in the *San Francisco Examiner &*

Chronicle (December 27, 1970), p. 2. The USAF "vegetation control" announcement was cited in "A Technology Assessment," p. 17.

Hushed Mangroves

Mangroves and hydroseres are described in P. W. Richards' classic study of tropical forest ecology, *The Tropical Rain Forest* (London: Cambridge University Press, 1952), pp. 283–302. Swamp forests of South Vietnam are discussed in Llewelyn Williams, *Forests of Southeast Asia, Puerto Rico, and Texas* (Washington, D.C.: USDA CR 12–67, 1967), pp. 111–19. Mangrove succession is outlined by Fred H. Tschirley in "Defoliation in Vietnam," *Science*, vol. 163 (February 21, 1969), pp. 781–82.

Tschirley's estimate of the percentage of mangroves killed by one herbicide application is from Richard D. McCarthy, *The Ultimate Folly* (New York: Knopf, 1969), p. 89. Gordon H. Orians and E. W. Pfeiffer reported on mangroves in "Ecological Effects of the War in Vietnam," *Science*, vol. 168 (May 1, 1970), pp. 545–46. Dr. Pfeiffer kindly supplemented his published observations in conversations with me on December 5, 1970.

Spreading the Green Desert

Llewelyn Williams discusses reduction of Indochina's forests in *Forests of Southeast Asia, Puerto Rico, and Texas*, pp. 17–18; present forest extent is from page 5; the forest classification is presented on pages 61–66; and description of forest succession is from page 167. Description of evergreen forests is from P. W. Richards, *The Tropical Rain Forest*.

Effects of herbicides on South Vietnam's forests are viewed by Tschirley in "Defoliation in Vietnam," pp. 782–85; and by Orians and Pfeiffer, "Ecological Effects of the War in Vietnam," pp. 546–48. Richards was quoted by Tschirley concerning the Angkor forest.

The article by George R. Harvey and Jay D. Mann is "Picloram in Vietnam," which appeared in *Scientist and Citizen* (September 1968), pp. 165–71. The threatened future of the tropical rain forest is movingly described by Richards, *The Tropical Rain Forest*, pp. 404 ff. Dr. Arthur H. Westing mentioned "secondary climax" and estimated tree destruction in South Vietnam's dense forests in "Effects of Military Defoliation on the Forests of South Vietnam," invitational address before the American Association for the Advancement of Science at its 137th annual meeting, held in Chicago, December 29, 1970. The process of Saharization is discussed in the MRI Report, pp. 266–67.

Crop Destruction

The origins of the crop destruction program are traced in "A Technology Assessment," p. 11. Dr. Jean Mayer's article, "Starvation as a Weapon," is in Steven Rose (ed.), *Chemical and Biological Warfare*, pp. 76–85. Dr. Hornig is quoted in Richard D. McCarthy, *The Ultimate Folly*, p. 88.

Dr. Meselson's observations on the effects of crop spraying on civilians are reported in the *New York Times* (December 30, 1970), p. 1. The five US Army studies, which indicate that crop spraying harms civilians, not enemy troops, are summarized by Victor Cohn in the *San Francisco Chronicle* (December 31, 1970), p. 10. Carefully culled findings from two of these studies, which were presented by Rear Admiral William E. Lemos to a House of Representatives subcommittee, can be read in Thomas Whiteside, *Defoliation*, pp. 86–93.

Harvey and Mann describe the effects of picloram on food crops in "Picloram in Vietnam," p. 166. Orians and Pfeiffer describe "accidental" defoliation, crop destruction, and effects of herbicides on South Vietnam's rubber industry in "Ecological Effects of the War in Vietnam," pp. 549–53. Nguyen Thuoc of Dispatch News International reported damage to the National Park in an unpublished article, "Vietnam Massacre: Trees," June 1970.

H. G. Baker, *Plants and Civilization* (Belmont, Calif.: Wadsworth, 1970) discusses the importance of botanical gardens (pages 23–26) and tells the tale of the spread of rubber culture from its origin in Brazil (page 125–32). The international investigating group's studies in Cambodia resulted in the "Report on Herbicidal Damage by the United States in Southeastern Cambodia," by A. H. Westing, E. W. Pfeiffer, J. Lavorel, and L. Matarasso. It is printed in Thomas Whiteside, *Defoliation*, pp. 117–32.

Land Deform in the Mekong Delta

Clifford Geertz describes the ecology of rice paddies on pages 17–25 of his article, "Two Types of Ecosystems," in Andrew P. Vayda (ed.), *Environment and Cultural Behavior*. The amount of land abandoned owing to the war is estimated in the Joint Development Group's summarized report, *Postwar Development of Viet-Nam*, p. 18.

A revealing study of the agricultural economics of the Mekong delta is given in Robert L. Sansom, *The Economics of Insurgency in the Mekong Delta of Vietnam* (Cambridge, Mass.: MIT Press, 1970). My account is drawn mainly from Sansom's chapters entitled "Land and Income: A Historical Inquiry" and "Recent Conditions of Land Tenure." In his concluding chapter, "The Economics of Insurgency," Sansom contrasts the myths created by various counterinsurgent "scientists" with the realities of land and war he found in the Mekong delta.

Duong Son Quan's article, "Is the 'Land to the Tiller" Bill as Perfect as His Excellency Ambassador Bunker Claims?" appeared first in the Saigon magazine *Tu Quyet*, then in translated form in the October 1970 issue of *Thoi-Bao Ga*, edited by Ngo Vinh Long (76-A Pleasant Street, Cambridge, Mass. 02139).

Chapter 3: War upon the Animals

The flight of animals to Cambodia is mentioned in Thomas Whiteside, *Defoliation*, pp. 127-28. Orians and Pfeiffer discuss the effects of herbicides on Indochina's fauna in "Ecological Effects of the War in Vietnam," pp. 548-49.

The Stanford University biologists quoted are Lawrence E. Gilbert, Peter H. Raven, and Paul R. Ehrlich, from their letter to *Science*, vol. 161 (September 6, 1968), p. 964. Endangered animal species of Indochina are discussed by the MRI Report, pp. 267-69. Information on tropical plant-animal interdependence is from an unpublished paper by Lawrence E. Gilbert, graduate student in ecology at Stanford University, October 21, 1970.

Vietnamese testimony given at the Russell war-crimes tribunal about herbicide effects on plants, animals, and humans is cited in Seymour M. Hersh, *Chemical & Biological Warfare* (New York: Anchor Books, 1969), pp. 133-34. NLF claims are found in "Documents on Chemical Warfare Carried out in South Vietnam by the United States," presented to the 5th Stockholm Conference on Vietnam, March 1970.

The MRI Report reviews herbicide toxicity beginning on page 151: cacodylic acid, pp. 159-65; picloram, pp. 177-82; 2,4-D, pp. 189-95; and 2,4,5-T, pp. 196-98. Malathion spraying in South Vietnam is mentioned in the *New York Times* (December 30, 1970), p. 1. Toxicity of Malathion to honeybees is noted in

ECOLOGY OF DEVASTATION: INDOCHINA

"Toxicity of Pesticides and Other Agricultural Chemicals to Honey Bees," (Riverside, Calif.: University of California Agricultural Extension, July 1967), p. 3. The quotation about tigers is from the Orians and Pfeiffer article "Ecological Effects of the War in Vietnam," p. 553. William R. Corson reports on his fish-blasting expedition in *The Betrayal* (New York: Ace Books, 1968), pp. 165–67.

Chapter 4: The Lunarization Program

Orians and Pfeiffer discuss craterization in "Ecological Effects of the War in Vietnam," p. 552. News reports, such as the *San Francisco Chronicle* (November 21, 1970), p. 15, covered the heavy bombing of the Ho Chi Minh Trail in the latter months of 1970. A sensitive report of a large military operation in Vietnam is Jonathan Schell, *The Village of Ben Suc* (New York: Vintage, 1968); my quotation is from page 20.

Much of the analysis of military effects on the soil is from an unpublished paper by Clyde Wahrhaftig, Professor of Geology at the University of California in Berkeley, entitled "Some Possible Effects of Military Activity on Soils of Southeast Asia," 1970. Laterization is discussed in the MRI Report, pp. 281–84; Tschirley, "Defoliation in Vietnam," pp. 780–81; and a mimeographed paper by Gerardo Budowski, "Tropical Savannas, a Sequence of Forest Felling and Repeated Burning," 1956.

Cultivation of peaty soils is described in Thai Cong Tung, *Natural Environment and Land Use in South Vietnam* (Saigon: Ministry of Agriculture, 1967), p. 45 (this volume has a soil survey of all South Vietnam). Precipitation in Indochina is covered by M. Y. Nuttonson, *The Physical Environment and Agriculture of South Vietnam, Laos and Cambodia*, pp. 12–14. Nutrient cycling and soil conditions in a tropical forest are described by P. W. Richards, *The Tropical Rain Forest*, pp. 205–20.

The MRI Report discusses changes in climate attributable to land stripping on pages 284–87 and the effects of herbicides on soil microorganisms on pages 198–200.

Chapter 5: Airs, Waters, and Places: Environments of Disease

A work that explains environmental effects on human health—and much more—is René Dubos, *Man Adapting* (New Haven: Yale University Press, 1965). The quotations of Hippocrates come from pages 36–37 and page 62 of that book; the quotation of Dubos himself comes from page 169.

Civilian casualties in Indochina are discussed in the Senate Refugee Subcommittee's staff report, "Refugee Problems in Indochina." I have quoted from pages 11–13.

Poisons from the Airs

A summary of herbicide toxicity studies is in the MRI Report, pp. 151 ff. Scientific findings about 2,4,5-T are gathered in "The Effects of 2,4,5-T on Man and Environment." Hearings of the Subcommittee on Energy, Natural Resources and Environment, of the Commerce Committee, US Senate, 91st Congress, 2nd Session (April 7–15, 1970). Dr. Verrett's findings about the effects of 2,4,5-T and 2,4-D in chick embryos are reported on page 196 of that document.

The story of the concealment of the Bionetics Report is from an unpublished paper by Polly Roberts, an Associate of the Center for Study of Responsive Law, who was involved in the exposure of the report. The *Tin Sang* story about "monster fetuses" is translated in the *Yale Daily News* (December 2, 1969). Findings of the AAAS investigation team are reported in the *New York Times* (December 30, 1970), p. 1, but the quotation is from the unpublished Herbicide Assessment Commission Report). In his book, *Defoliation*, Thomas Whiteside estimates the amount of 2,4,5-T consumed by a pregnant Vietnamese woman on page 31 and discusses dioxin on pages 44–53. *Defoliation* also contains an account of the exposure of the Bionetics Report.

Orians and Pfeiffer note the effects of cacodylic acid on people in "Ecological Effects of the War in Vietnam," p. 549. Use of tear gas and nausea gas in Vietnam is described by Seymour M. Hersh, *Chemical & Biological Warfare*, pp. 142–59. The Harvard doctors and Dr. Vennema are quoted on pages 156–57 of Hersh's book.

Stagnant Waters and Unhealthy Places

The quotation of Frances FitzGerald is from pages 150–51 of her article, "The Tragedy of Saigon," in Barry Weisberg (ed.), *Ecocide in Indochina*. Malaria is discussed by René Dubos, *Man Adapting*, pp. 237 and 375. My account of malaria in Indochina is drawn mainly from an unpublished paper, "Pollution, Public Health and Nutrition Effects of Mekong Basin Hydro-Development" (1970), by John P. Milton of The Conservation Foundation, 1717 Massachusetts Avenue NW, Washington, D.C. 20036.

ECOLOGY OF DEVASTATION: INDOCHINA

The plague epidemic in South Vietnam is reported by Seymour M. Hersh, *Chemical & Biological Warfare*, pp. 159–60. The VD pandemic in America was reported in the *San Francisco Chronicle* (November 16, 1970), p. 9.

Chapter 6: Environments of Technocratic War

Arthur W. Galston's proposed ban on ecocide is mentioned in Barry Weisberg (ed.), *Ecocide in Indochina*, p. 4. Jean-Paul Sartre's essay "On Genocide" is also in that volume, beginning on page 33. Withdrawal of the Special Forces from Vietnam is reported in the *San Francisco Chronicle* (January 5, 1971), p. 12.

The excerpt from *The New Yorker* is from Noam Chomsky, *At War With Asia*, p. 78. Quotations from René Dubos' excellent discussion of evolution in his book, *Man, Medicine and Environment* (New York: Mentor, 1968), are from pages 10–11 and page 50. For a view of man as a pioneer or climax species, see F. R. Fosberg, "The Preservation of Man's Environment," in Paul Shepard and Daniel McKinley (eds.), *The Subversive Science*, p. 335.

Technocracy at War

The interbureaucratic struggles of Laos are untangled by Peter Dale Scott, "Air America: Flying the U.S. into Laos," in Nina S. Adams and Alfred W. McCoy (eds.), *Laos: War and Revolution*, pp. 301–21. On pages 149–50 of Jonathan Schell's fine book, *The Military Half*, there is an Orwellian military list of rounds expended and targets annihilated.

Seymour Melman, *Pentagon Capitalism* (New York: McGraw-Hill, 1970), provides the best analysis of the Defense Department system I have seen. Melman describes Pentagon budget growth on page 22, percentage of the GNP it consumes on page 10, defines the state-management's growth drive on page 16, and tells the tonnage of explosives dropped on the two Vietnams on page 143.

Hoopes and Katzenbach are quoted by the *San Francisco Chronicle* (January 6, 1971), p. 11. For a history of the Sheridan super not-quite-a-tank from misconception to obsolescence, see Ward Just, "Soldiers, Part II," in *The Atlantic Monthly* (November 1970), pp. 59–68. Just presents the annual H&I rate on page 84.

Conversion to the Heavy Metal State is remarked by William S. Burroughs, *The Soft Machine* (New York: Evergreen Black

Cat, 1967), pp. 162–63. I think the best novel of the Second Indochina War is Burroughs' *The Ticket That Exploded* (New York: Evergreen Black Cat, 1968).

Energy Sources

A study of the war's impact on the American economy is Robert Eisner, "The War and the Economy," in Sam Brown and Len Ackland (eds.), *Why Are We Still in Vietnam?* (New York: Vintage, 1970), pp. 109–23; my quotations are from pages 110–11, page 113, and page 120. Seymour Melman, in *Pentagon Capitalism*, defines "new imperialism" on page 34, rejects Marxist analysis on page 156, describes the Defense Department and its contractors as a single management system throughout the book (see especially pages 156 and 181), tells the cost of killing an Indochinese on page 144, and notes on page 74 that the Pentagon will find use for the money freed by ending the war.

The *San Francisco Examiner & Chronicle* (January 10, 1971), p. 2, printed Defense Department war-casualty figures. The popular press continues to cover the decay of the US Army in South Vietnam.

The Spectrum of Threats

Secretary Laird's statement on "the spectrum of threats" is cited by Ward Just, "Soldiers, Part II," p. 69. Seymour Melman notes the Pentagon's lobbying effort in *Pentagon Capitalism*, p. 175, and debunks concepts of so-called deterrence and overkill throughout his book. Mr. Downer's statement appears in Noam Chomsky, *At War With Asia*, pp. 24–25.

Kenneth E. Boulding discusses the mutation of ideas in "Economics and Ecology," in F. Fraser Darling and John P. Milton (eds.), *Future Environments of North America* (Garden City, N Y.: The Natural History Press, 1966), pp. 228–29. Representative McCarthy documents Congressional ignorance of military programs in his book *The Ultimate Folly*, pp. 126–27. One of many news reports on military intelligence-gathering in America is in the *San Francisco Chronicle* (January 19, 1971), p. 11.

Chapter 7: Switchboard Devastation

Ward Just describes STANO in "Soldiers, Part II," pp. 84–86. For a discussion of new trends in training military counterinsurgency advisers, see Just's article, pp. 72–75. Quotations of Westmoreland's "automated battlefield" oration are from John

Dower, "Ten Points of Note: Asia and the Nixon Doctrine," in *The Bulletin of Concerned Asian Scholars*, vol. 2, no. 4 (Fall 1970), pp. 56–57 [the full address is in *Congressional Record* (October 16, 1969).] Dower discusses the C-5A jet transport on page 55, cites an estimate of nuclear weapons in Southeast Asia on page 59, and quotes Nixon and Hanson Baldwin on nuclear weapons on pages 58–60. [Baldwin's article, "After Vietnam—What Military Strategy in the Far East?" is in *The New York Times Magazine* (June 9, 1968).]

The planned depopulation of the I Corps region is reported in the *San Francisco Chronicle* (January 11, 1971), p. 1. Seek Data II and the sensor-sealed border plan are mentioned in Derek Shearer, "Automated War," in Barry Weisberg, (ed.), *Ecocide in Indochina*, pp. 188–89. Fred Branfman mentions Project Alpha in "Laos: 'No Place to Hide,'" *The Bulletin of Concerned Asian Scholars* (Fall 1970), p. 29. George McArthur's report, "'Spook Line' in Delta Cuts Red Infiltration," is in the *Los Angeles Times* (October 22, 1970), p. 1. The B-57 program is reported in the *San Francisco Chronicle* (January 19, 1971), p. 13.

Discussion of the SIU center is based on Jonathan Mirsky, "The Carbondale Caper," in *The Bulletin of Concerned Asian Scholars* (Fall 1970), pp. 71–73. The *San Francisco Chronicle* (January 19, 1971) ran Michael Maclear's article on the reconstruction program in North Vietnam on page 13 and reported growing American military involvement in Cambodia on page 1. The *Los Angeles Times*, February 25, 1971, reported the supply of Thai mercenaries to the clandestine army on page 6, and on page 7 printed Thieu's "when we fight pirates" statement. On February 26, 1971, the *San Francisco Chronicle*, page 13, reported Thieu's predicted invasion of North Vietnam. Daniel Lang explores the unthinkable in "A Reporter at Large (Atomic Bombs)," *The New Yorker* (January 9, 1971), pp. 52–61.

Index

A Shau Valley, 74
ABC Committee, 61
Abiotic elements, 103, 104–105
Acidic soils, 106
Action Platoon (CAP), 35
Advanced Research Projects
  Agency (ARPA), 83
Agency for International Development (AID), 34, 134, 150
Agent Blue, 63–64, 68, 81, 100, 101, 118
Agent Orange, 63–64, 75–77, 84, 96, 99, 100, 109, 114–117
Agent Purple, 63–64, 75, 100
Agent White, 63–64, 68, 75, 76, 79, 81, 84, 115
Agriculture
  Cambodia, 22, 45, 86, 87; slash-and-burn, 43
  Indochina, 19, 24–25, 60–61; revolution fostered by France, 22–23; slash-and-burn (swidden), 20–21, 37, 71, 79, 80, 82
  Laos, 61; opium, 38, 39; slash-and-burn, 37
  North Vietnam, 53–54, 55
  South Vietnam, 58, 61, 79, 80, 104–105; crop destruction, 81–88
  U.S., 62
  Vietnam, 22–23
Agrovilles, 25
Air America, 134
Air Force and Space Digest, 149
Albert, Carl, 144
American Association for the Advancement of Science (AAAS), 66, 73, 79, 82–83, 97, 101, 117, 118, 145; Herbicide Assessment Commission, 60, 70, 77, 81, 87, 117
American Community Association, 42

American Social Health Association, 124
Ammonification, 108
Amoebiasis, 123
Ancestor-worship, 30
Angkor, 11–12, 45
Angkor Wat, 11, 78, 106
Animals, 95–102; as decomposers, 96; forest defoliation and, 96–98; plant interdependence, 96–98; toxicity of defoliants, 96, 98–99, 100
Animism, 30, 56
Annam, protectorate of, 22
Annam Cordillera, 19
Ansul Chemical Company, 100
Apatite, 54
Aquatic fauna, 96–97
Arsenical insecticides, 100–101
Assessment of Ecological Effects of Extensive or Repeated Use of Herbicides (the MRI Report), 59–60, 63, 65, 99, 100, 101, 106, 108–109, 113–114
Attopeu, 41
Avicennia marina, 69

Baldwin, Hanson, 152–153
Bamboo, 72–73, 78–79, 80
Bao Dai, 23
Batangan Peninsula, 35
Bees, 97, 101
Bien Dien Phu, 24
Bien Hoa airbase, 85
Binh Long, 75
Bioclimatic system, 72
Bionetics Laboratory, 115–116
Birds, 96–98
Birth control, 55–56
Black-market, 49
Boloven plateau, 18, 150
Bombing; Cambodia, 104; Laos, 39–40, 104; North Vietnam, 12, 33, 38, 40, 53, 54–55, 56,

169

INDEX

104, 151; South Vietnam, 103–109
Boulding, Kenneth E., 143–144
Branfman, Fred, 40–41
British Malaya, 16, 32
Brown, J. W., 62–63
Bruguiera parviflora, 69
Bubonic plague, 123
Buddhism, 30, 44, 50; geomancers, 30
Buell, Edgar, 38, 39
Buffaloes, 95
Bureaucracy, 133–138
Burma, 28
Burroughs, William S., 133, 137–138

Ca Mau peninsula, 70, 106
Cacodylic acid, 63, 64, 100, 101
Cam Ranh Base, U.S. lease on, 36
Cam Ranh Bay area, 35, 36
Cambodia, 11, 12, 19, 20, 23, 27–28, 41, 43–47, 57, 68, 74, 78, 130, 140, 150, 151
  agriculture, 22, 45, 86, 87; slash-and-burn, 43
  bombing of, 104
  defoliation, 87, 95
  economy, 43, 45, 87
  France in, 44, 46; establishes protectorate over, 21–22
  population, 44
  refugees, 36
  soil, 105
  U.S. aid to, 46
Cambodian National Assembly, 43
Camp Drum, 62
Canals, 90, 99
Cap St. Jacques, 70
Carcinogenic compounds, 100–101
Cardamon Mountains, 74
Carnivores, 58, 60
Carson, Rachel, 114
Catholics, 31, 52
Center for International Affairs, 87

Center for Study of Responsible Law, 115–116, 118–119
Central Intelligence Agency (CIA), 25, 26–28, 31, 38, 52, 134, 135, 144, 151
Central Minorities School, 24
Ceriops candolleana, 69
Chaliand, Gérard, 55, 56
Cham civilization, 11, 12, 19, 124, 125, 126
Chao Phraya River basin, 19
Chevalier, 78
China, 19, 37–38, 39, 53
Cholera, 123
CINCPAC, 83–84
Civil Operations Revolutionary Development Support (CORDS), 135
Civilian Irregular Defense Groups (CIDG), 26
Clandestine Army, 38, 39, 41, 134
Coal, 54
Cochin China (colony), 22
Coffee, 22
Communism, 16, 38, 45, 46, 48, 129, 134, 151, 152; on herbicide use, 67
Conference on War and National Responsibility, 128
Confucianism, 30
Coniferous forests, 73, 79
Conscription; South Vietnam, 48; U.S., 142
Conservation Foundation, 122
Cooperatives, 53–54
Copper Basin, 108
Corn, 38
Corson, Colonel William R., 102
Counterinsurgency, 16–17, 29, 32, 33, 65, 90, 111; importance of plants to, 58–59
Craters, 103–104, 106–107, 121
Crop destruction, 81–88

Darlac plateau, 73, 79
Darling, F. Fraser, 17–18
Darwin, Charles, 131

INDEX

Dau, Truong, 85–86
DDT, 110, 117, 121–122
Deciduous forests, 74
Decomposers, 58, 60; animals as, 96
Decornoy, Jacques, 39, 42–43, 47
Decree 57, 92
Defoliants, 61–68; as toxic to animals, 96, 98–99, 100; *See also* names of defoliants
Defoliation, 14, 87, 95
  crop destruction, 81–88
  forest, 58–59, 65–81, 107–108; animals and, 96–98; windrift from, 87
Delmore, F. J., 68
Demilitarized Zone, 31, 65, 149
Democratic Republic of Vietnam, *see* North Vietnam
Devastation Model, 33, 36
2, 4-Dichlorophenoxyacetic acid (2, 4-D), 61–64, 79, 99–100, 108–109, 113–115, 117, 118
Dicotyledonous trees, 80
Diem, Ngo Dinh, 24, 30–31, 32, 91, 92
Dinh, 30
Dioxin, 117–118
Dipterocarp forests, 73, 98
Disease, 82, 110–127; Montagnards, 125–126; refugees and, 120, 121
Dispatch News International, 28, 85
Dogs, killing of, 95
Douc langurs, 97
Dow Chemical Company, 116
Downer, Samuel F., 143
Dresser, Major Ralph, 67
Dubos, René, 111, 121, 122, 131–133
Duc, Ngo Cong, 53
Dudman, Richard, 47

Ecocide, 128–129
Ecology; defined, 13; as a field of study, 15; guidelines for the study of, 17–18; teamwork in, 18
Economics of Insurgency, The (Sansom), 90
Economy
  Cambodia, 43, 45, 87
  Indochina, 19–21, 29–30
  North Vietnam, 89
  South Vietnam, 48–49, 89–90
  U.S., 129, 138–140
Ecosystems, 15; studies of, 60–61
Education; North Vietnam, 55; South Vietnam, 24
Eisner, Robert, 139
Electronic surveillance, 149–150
Epstein, Dr. Samuel, 115
Erosion, 106, 107
Euglossine bees, 97
Evergreen forests, 73–75, 79, 80, 97
Evolution, 131–133

FAK, 47
Filariasis, 123
Fire-climax savannas, 80
First Defoliation Conference, 63
First Indochina War, 23–25, 29; beginning of, 23
Fish, 98, 99, 102
FitzGerald, Frances, 120
Flamm, Dr. Barry, 77
Fleas, 123
Floristic system, 72
Food and Drug Administration (FDA), 115, 116
Food-denial program, 81–82
Food-for-Peace program, 137
Forces Armées Royales Khmers (FARK), 43–46
Foreign Affairs, 37
Forests, 60
  bioclimatic associations, 72
  classification of, 72, 73
  coniferous, 73, 79
  deciduous, 74

INDEX

defoliation, 58–59, 65–81, 107–108; animals and, 96–98; wind-drift from, 87
dipterocarp, 73, 98
evergreen, 73–75, 79, 80, 97
mangroves, 69–71, 96, 107
monsoon, 73
montane, 73
nutrients of, 20–21
percentage of land covered by, 71
regeneration, 78–80
seasonal, 73, 74, 75–77, 80, 97
secondary, 71
semideciduous, 73
tropical rain, 74, 77–78
Fort Detrick, 62, 74, 79
Fosberg, F. R., 133
France, 11–12, 26, 53, 90, 148
  agricultural revolution fostered by, 22–23
  in Cambodia, 44, 46; establishes protectorate over, 21–22
  colonization, 21–23
  First Indochina War, 23
  in Laos, 37; establishes protectorate over, 21–22
  Siam cedes Laos to, 22
  splits Vietnam into three administrative units, 22
  Vietnam declares independence from, 23
Free-strike zones, 33–34
French Indochina, 12
Front Uni National Kampuchea (FUNK), 47
Fulbright, J. William, 150
Fulro, 27–28

Galston, Arthur W., 128
Gas; nausea, 119; tear, 119
Geertz, Clifford, 89–90
General Dynamics Corporation, 140
Geneva Convention, 24, 128
Genocide, 128
Giap, Vo Nguyen, 23

Gold, 41
Great Britain, 32; vegetational biomass, 60
Greece, 137
Green Berets, 144, 149
Guerrillas; North Vietnam, 53; South Vietnam, 29, 31

Haiphong, 54
Halang tribe, 43
Hannah, Dr. John A., 34–36, 150
Hanoi, 23, 54, 56
Harassment-and-interdiction (H&I), 33
Harvard University, 37, 60, 87, 115, 119
Harvey, Frank, 67
Harvey, George R., 79, 84, 85
Health, 119–124
Hemorrhagic fever, 123
Herbicides, 59–60, 75, 79, 130; communists on use of, 67; effects on humans, 98, 113–118; Operation Ranch Hand, 61–68; U.S. production of, 62; use in U.S., 114; *See also* names of herbicides
Herbivores, 58, 60
Hippocrates, 110–111
Ho Chi Minh, 23, 25, 53
Ho Chi Minh Trail, 65, 74, 104, 130, 149
Ho Nai, 85
Hollistic system, 72
Hoopes, Townsend, 136
Hornig, Donald F., 82
Hou Youn, 44
Huk movement, 16, 31
Humans; herbicide effects, 98, 113–118; pesticide effects, 114–116
Huntington, Samuel P., 36–37, 43, 48

I Corps, 148–149
Iba Ham, 27
Immigrants, 19; *See also* Refugees

INDEX

Import duties, 50
Indochina
  agriculture, 19, 24–25, 60–61; revolution fostered by France, 22–23; slash-and-burn (swidden), 20–21
  alluvial plains of, 21
  economy, 19–21, 29–30
  ethnic groups of, 20
  first U.S. aid to, 25
  history, 18–24
  immigrants, 19
  irrigation, 19, 21, 22; system in Red River delta, 22
  monsoons, 19, 20, 106, 107
  mountain tribes, 18–29
  population, 21
  size of, 18
  topography, 20
  valley kingdoms, 19–29
  See also names of countries
Indochinese gibbons, 97
Industry, 54, 55, 56
Insecticides, 100–101
Insurgency, 16–17; importance of plants to, 58–59
International Voluntary Services (IVS), 36, 121, 122
Iron, 54
Iron Triangle, 74, 104
Irrigation, 19, 21, 22; system in Red River delta, 22

Japan, 23, 53
Jarai tribe, 43
Jews, 128
Johnson, Anita, 115
Johnson, Lyndon B., 40
Joint Development Group, 51, 61, 90
Joint Strategic Operating Plan, 136
Just, Ward, 146
Jute, 25

Karen tribesmen, 28
Katzenbach, Nicholas, 137

Keptospirosis, 123
Khmer Loeu, 43–44, 47
Khmer Range, 43–44, 47
Khmers, 11, 19, 20
King, Dr. Martin Luther, 147
Korea, 31, 32
Korean Model, 31
Kraus, E. J., 61–62
Ky, Nguyen Cao, 56

Laird, Melvin, 142
Lan Xang kingdom, 19–20
Land reform; North Vietnam, 53; South Vietnam, 89–94
Landlord system, 61
Lang, Daniel, 153
Languages, 24; the Raglai, 124
Lao, the, 19
Laos, 12, 18, 20, 23, 29, 37–43, 57, 74, 134, 135, 150, 151
  agriculture, 61; opium, 38, 39; slash-and-burn, 37
  amount of forests in, 71
  bombing of, 39–40, 104
  Clandestine Army, 38, 39, 41, 134
  France in, 37; establishes protectorate over, 21–22
  refugees, 29, 36, 39, 40–41, 42, 104
  Siam cedes to France, 22
  soil, 105
  two cultures of, 41–42
  U.S. aid to, 41
Lateritic soils, 11–12, 105–106
Lemkin, Raphael, 128
Lifton, Robert Jay, 51
Lillienthal, David E., 51
Liver fluke, 123
Lobbyists, 142–143
Lockheed Corporation, 140
Lon Nol, 43, 44, 46, 47
Long Cheng, 151
Los Angeles Times, 149
LTV Aerospace Corporation, 143
Luce, Don, 48
Lundbord, Louis B., 139

173

INDEX

McArthur, George, 149–150
McCarthy, Richard D., 144
McNamara Line, 31, 149
Macroclimate, 108
Mailer, Norman, 133
Maize, 38
Malaria, 120–123
Malaria pills, 122–123
Malathion, 101, 118–119, 121
Malayan Model, 32
Malnutrition, 82
Mangroves, 69–71, 96, 107
Mann, Jay D., 79, 84, 85
Mao Tse-tung, 29
Marijuana, 42
Matak, Sirik, 43
Mayer, Dr. Jean, 82
Mekong River, 11, 45, 46, 49
Mekong River delta, 12, 18, 19, 20, 22, 38, 65, 67, 148–149; defoliation in, 84–85, 96; land reform in, 89–94; malaria in, 121; mangroves in, 69–71; population, 91; rice, 89–90, 93; soil, 106
Melaleuca leucadendron, 69
Melman, Seymour, 136, 140
Meo tribesmen, 20, 21, 37–38, 39, 41, 134, 151
Meselson, Dr. Matthew S., 60, 82–83, 115, 117
Miconia species, 97–98
Microorganisms, 108
Midwest Research Institute, 59
Mike Force units, 26, 27, 50
Milton, John P., 122, 123
Minarik, Dr. C. E., 79
Ming, Duong Van, 52–53
Mining, 54
Mon tribesmen, 28
Monde, Le, 39
Mon-Khmer, the, 20
Monsoon forests, 73
Monsoons, 19, 20, 106, 107
Montagnards, 25, 26, 68, 82–83, 88, 95, 109; disease, 125–126; the Raglai, 124–126

Montane forests, 73
Morrow, Michael, 28
Mosquitoes, 120–122
Mountain tribes, 18–29
MRI Report, *see Assessment of Ecological Effects of Extensive or Repeated Use of Herbicides*
Muong, the, 20
My Ca, 36
My Lai massacre, 68

Nakhorn Phanom, 149
National Academy of Sciences, 145
National Cancer Institute, 114–115
National Liberation Front (NLF), 26, 27, 28, 32, 33, 35, 43–48, 52, 65, 66, 70, 71, 74, 82, 83, 91, 93, 95, 98, 114, 124–126, 135, 141, 152, 153
National Liberation Front-North Vietnamese Army (NLF-NVA), 34, 44–46, 83
Nausea gas, 119
Nazi Germany, 128
Neak Leong, 46
New York Times, The, 149, 152
New Yorker, The, 131
Nghe An, 53
Ngiem, Thai Lang, 51–52
Nhu, Ngo Dinh, 31, 32
19th Parallel, 40
Nipa fruticans, 69
Nipa palm, 69
Nitrification, 108
Nitrogen fixation, 108
Nixon, Richard M., 51, 68, 130, 141, 152
Noösphere, 16
North Vietnam, 18–19, 20, 24, 26, 39, 40, 41, 48, 53–57, 65, 130, 141, 142, 153; agriculture, 53–54, 55; amount of forests in, 71; animism, 56; birth-control campaign, 55–56; bombing of, 12, 33, 38, 40, 53, 54–55, 56, 104, 151;

174

cooperatives, 53–54; economy, 89; education, 55; First Indochina War, 23; guerrillas, 53; industry, 54, 55, 56; land reform, 53; medical services, 55; mining, 54; propaganda, 56; refugees, 31; sanitation, 55; *See also* South Vietnam; Vietnam
North Vietnamese Army (NVA), 33, 54–55
Nuclear weapons, 143, 152–153
Nungs, 125

Office of Strategic Services (OSS), 25
Open Arms amnesty program, 31
Operation Cedar Falls, 104
Operation Dufflebag, 150
Operation Ranch Hand (Hades), 61–68
Operation Russell Beach, 35
Opium, 38, 39
Orians, Gordon H., 70–71, 86, 96, 98, 99–100, 101, 118

Paragonimiasis, 123
Pathet Lao (PL), 38–39, 42, 47
Pesticides, 114–116
Pfeiffer, Dr. E. W., 70–71, 77, 80–81, 86–87, 96, 98–101, 118, 145
Philippine Model, 31
Philippines, 16, 32, 112
Phong Bac, 102
Phou Tha Thi, 38, 40
Phouma, Souvanna, 151
Physiognomic system, 72
Picloram, 63, 76, 79, 100, 108–109
Plague, 123
Plain of Jars, 18, 40–41, 104
Plants, 58–94, 107; animal interdependence, 96–98; classification of, 58; importance of, 58–59; Operation Ranch Hand, 61–68; pollination, 97; seed dispersal, 97–98

Plasmodium falciparum, 122
Pnom Penh, 44, 45, 46, 47
Pdzolic soils, 106
Pollination, 97
Popkin, Samuel, 87–88
Population, 15; Cambodia, 44; Indochina, 21; Saigon, 47; South Vietnam, 26, 34, 91; Vietnam, 23
Producer level, 58
Project Alpha, 149
Provincial Reconnaisance Units (PRU), 27
Proxmire, William, 136, 137
Puerto Rico, 74, 75, 77, 79

Quan, Duong Son, 92–93, 94
Quang Nam, 112
Quang Ngai, 68, 112
Quang Tin, 68
Quang Tri, 112
Questionnaires, 18

Rach Gia, 106
Raglai, the, 124–126
Rainfall, 73–74, 106–108; Spain, 108
Ramie, 25
Rand Corporation, 83
Rats, 123
Red River delta, irrigation system in, 22
Red River valley, 19, 23
Refugees; Cambodia, 36; disease and, 120, 121; Laos, 29, 36, 39, 40–41, 42, 104; North Vietnam, 31; South Vietnam, 30–31, 32, 33, 34, 35, 82, 95, 124–126
Religion, 11, 30–31, 44, 50, 52
Revolutionary Development Cadres, 31
Rhizophora conjugata, 69
Rice, 19–22, 45, 59, 67, 71, 84, 85; destruction of stores of, 81–82; Mekong delta, 89–90,

INDEX

93; new strains of, 61; toxic residues on, 101
Richards, P. W., 78, 81
Ridenhour, Ronald, 115
Roberts, Polly, 118–119
Rome plows, 104
Royal Laotian Government (RLG), 38
Rubber, 22, 43, 44, 45, 86–87
Rubber Research Institute, 86
Rung Sat Peninsula, 70, 96
Rusk, Dean, 153
Russell war-crimes tribunal, 98

Saharization, 80
Saigon, 47–53, 74; black-market, 49; civil order, 47–48; corruption, 49–50; defoliation in, 85–86; economy, 48–49; health conditions in, 120; inflation, 50; municipal budget, 48; population, 47; sanitary conditions, 47; slums, 48
Saigon River, 70
Saline soils, 106
Sam Neua Province, 42
Sam Thong, 134
Sansom, Robert L., 90–92, 93
Saravane, 41
Savannas, 80–81
Schell, Jonathan, 104
Schistosomiasis, 123
Science, divisions of, 16
Scigliano, Robert, 25
Search-and-destroy operations, 33
Sears, Paul B., 14
Seasonal forests, 73, 74, 75–77, 79, 80, 97
Second Indochina War, *see* North Vietnam; South Vietnam; United States of America
Secondary forests, 71
Seed dispersal, 97–98
Seek Data II, 149
Semideciduous forests, 73
17th Parallel, 24, 31

Shan tribesmen, 28
Shiva (Hindu god), 11
Siam, 19, 20; cedes Laos to France, 22
Siem Reap, 45
Sihanouk, Norodom, 43, 44, 45, 47, 74
Silent Spring (Carson), 114
Slash-and-burn (swidden) agriculture, 20–21, 37, 71, 79, 80, 82; Cambodia, 43; Laos, 37
Social Darwinism, 131–132
Soil, 103–109; acidic, 106; Cambodia, 105; Laos, 105; lateritic, 11–12, 105–106; podzolic, 106; saline, 106; South Vietnam, 103–109
Soil microorganisms, 108
South Vietnam, 18–19, 29–37, 45, 47–53, 57
  agriculture, 58, 61, 79, 80, 104–105; crop destruction, 81–88
  amount of forests in, 71
  animal destruction, 95–102
  bombing of, 103–109
  casualties; civilian, 111–112; U.S., 141
  conscription, 48
  craters, 103–104, 106–107, 121
  defoliated forests, 58–59, 65–81
  economy, 48–49, 89–90
  education, 24
  ethnic groups, 26
  free-strike zones, 33–34
  guerrillas, 29, 31
  harassment-and-interdiction, 33
  health conditions in, 119–124
  human herbicide effects, 98, 113–118
  land reform, 89–94
  landlord system, 61
  mangroves, 69–71, 96, 107
  medical facilities, 112
  nausea gas use, 119
  Operation Ranch Hand, 61–68
  political prisoners, 48
  population, 26, 34, 91

176

refugees, 30–31, 32, 33, 34, 35, 82, 95, 124–126
search-and-destroy operations, 33
soil, 103–109
squirrel hunts, 33–34
tear gas use, 119
technocratic war, 128–145
transportation, 85
troop withdrawal from, 130, 142, 148
turkey shoots, 33–34
urbanization of, 34, 36–37
vegetational biomass, 60
See also North Vietnam; Vietnam

South Vietnamese Army (ARVN), 27, 35, 45, 46, 49
South Vietnamese Government (GVN), 25, 26, 27, 28, 35, 48, 49, 51, 52, 91, 93, 112, 125, 126, 152; import duty income, 50
Southern Illinois University, 150–151
Spain, 108
Spencer, Herbert, 132
Squirrel hunts, 33–34
Stanford University, 97
STANO concept, 146, 149
Stewart, Franklin, 148
Stone, General William, 83
Strategic Hamlet Program, 32
Swidden agriculture, *see* Slash-and-burn agriculture

Taiwan, 112
Tan Hoi, 116
Tan Son Nhut Airbase, 67, 101
Taxes, 82; U.S., 139
Tay Ninh, 75, 76, 117
Tea, 22
Tear gas, 119
Technocratic war, 128–145
Teilhard de Chardin, Pierre, 15
Temperatures, 107–108

Tennessee, 108
Tet offensive (1968), 48, 152
2,3,6,7-Tetrachlorodibenzo-p-dioxin, 117–118
Texas, 75
Thailand, 37, 38, 39, 75, 134, 149, 150, 151; amount of forests in, 71
Thieu, Nguyen Van, 45, 49, 50, 51, 56, 151–152; land-reform, 92–93
Tho tribesmen, 23
Thompson, Sir Robert, 32
Thuc, Vu Quoc, 51
Thuoc, Nguyen, 85–86
Tin, 54
Tin Sang, 116
Tonkin (North Vietnam, protectorate of), 22
Tonle Sap, 20
Transportation, 85
Traplining fauna, 97
2,4,5-Trichlorophenoxyacetic acid (2,4,5-T), 14, 62–64, 76, 79, 100, 108–109, 114, 115, 117
Trigger factors, 13–14
Trinidad, 97–98
Tropical rain forests, 74, 77–78
Trung, Ly Chanh, 52
Truong Son cadre program, 26–27
Tschirley, Fred H., 70, 78, 79, 106
Tu Duc, 85
Tu Quyet, 92
Tungsten, 54
Turkey shoots, 33–34
Typhoid, 123

Ubon Air Base, 150
Union of Soviet Socialist Republics, 143
United Nations, 128
United States of America
agriculture, 62
aid to Burma, 28
aid to Cambodia, 46
aid to Laos, 41
animal destruction, 95–102

177

INDEX

bombing; Cambodia, 104; Laos, 39–40, 104; North Vietnam, 12, 33, 38, 40, 53, 54–55, 56, 104, 151; South Vietnam, 103–109
casualties, 141
CIA, 25, 26–28, 31, 38, 52, 134, 135, 144, 151
cost of war, 139–140
counterinsurgency tactics, 16–17
creation of tribal armies, 26
crop destruction, 81–88
disease effects, 110–127
the draft, 142
ecocide by, 128–129
economy, 129, 138–140
first military aid in Indochina, 25
forest defoliation, 58–59, 65–81, 107–108
free-strike zones, 33–34
Green Berets, 144, 149
harassment-and-interdiction, 33
herbicide production, 62
herbicide use in, 114
lease on Cam Ranh Base, 36
lobbyists, 142–143
nuclear weapons, 143, 152–153
Operation Ranch Hand, 61–68
search-and-destroy operations, 33
squirrel hunts, 33–34
taxes, 139
technocratic war, 128–145
troop withdrawal, 130, 142, 148
turkey shoots, 33–34
vegetational biomass, 60
U.S. Army Chemical and Nuclear Operations, 83, 86
U.S. Department of Agriculture, 70
U.S. Department of Defense, 16, 38, 59, 60, 63, 65, 66, 68, 79, 80, 115, 138, 140, 142–145; budget, 136; electronic surveillance programs, 149–150

U.S. Health, Education, and Welfare Department (HEW), 114–116
U.S. Senate Refugee Subcommittee, 34–35, 36, 39, 41, 111–112
U.S. Special Forces, 26
University of California in Berkeley, 105
University of Chicago, 61–62
University of Saigon, 85
Uranium, 54
USAID, 77, 120
USDA Agriculture Handbook, 100, 332

Valley kingdoms, 18–29
Vang Pao, 38–39, 41, 134, 151
Vegetational biomass, 60
Venereal disease, 123–124
Vennema, Dr. Alje, 119
Verrett, Dr. Jacqueline, 115, 117, 118
Vientiane, 41
Viet Cong, 37, 91–92
Viet Minh, 23–24, 53, 91
Vietnam, 19, 20, 23; agriculture, 22–23; declares independence from France, 23; population, 23; the 17th Parallel, 24, 31; split into three administrative units, 22; *See also* North Vietnam; South Vietnam
Vietnam War, *see* North Vietnam; South Vietnam; United States of America
Vinh Cam, 36
Vung Tau, 70

Wahrhaftig, Clyde, 105, 106
Weather cycle, 108
West Germany, 117
Westing, Dr. Arthur H., 66, 73, 79–80, 97, 101, 118

178

Westmoreland, General William C., 146, 147, 149
Wheat, new strains of, 61
Whiteside, Thomas, 116
Williams, Llewelyn, 72, 77–78
World Council of Churches, 48
World Health Organization (WHO), 120, 123

World War II, 138

Xerji, Tim, 121
Xieng Khouang province, 37
Xom Chua, 48

Yale University, 128

Ziegler, Ronald, 68

WIDENER UNIVERSITY-WOLFGRAM LIBRARY

CIR   DS557.A68 L46
Ecology of devastation: Indochina.

3 3182 00210 2199